Praise for *The Unseen Companion*

This is so much more than another heroic story of overcoming tragedy and difficulty. Michelle elevates God's story above her own. She focuses so clearly how God showed up in every plot twist in her own story. She has written a book that goes beyond hope and inspiration to actually bring the reader closer to God. The reader will find a path to follow to manage emotions, overcome hurt, and allow God to supply all needs. I recommend this book to every woman who wants to recognize the voice and handprint of God in her everyday life.

NANCY KARPENSKE
Women's Pastor, LifeBridge Christian Church, Longmont, CO

I'm making a long list of single and married women and I will be giving them this book. In a beautiful, tender way, Michelle has brought the heart of all women to the throne room of Truth! Thank you for sharing your heart and leading us through Scripture in such a revealing and hopeful path of courage and hope!

YVETTE MAHER
Executive Pastor: Community and Women, New Life Church,
Colorado Springs

Michelle has walked the journey and understands the hardships that many single mothers face. She now has the passion to use that experience to encourage single mothers to find their hope and strength in Christ. It can be done, and she wants to show you how. Single mom, allow the pages of *The Unseen Companion* to bless you!

JENNIFER MAGGIO
Founder/CEO, The Life of a Single Mom Ministries,
www.thelifeofasinglemom.com

Our journey of ministering to women began thirty-three years ago and during that time we have seen first-hand the pain and suffering that single moms go through with courage and fortitude. *The Unseen Companion* fills a much-needed role for those brave women building a family single-handedly. We encourage the 2,500 pregnancy centers in our nation to make this book a gift they give to all the brave single mothers who choose life for their baby.

RAUL AND CHRISTINE REYES
President and Executive Director, CPC of Greater P

In a world of mixed messages that only offer false hope, Michelle Senters empowers single mothers and their children to *intentionally* rebuild and restore their lives and legacy with this very helpful and much-needed book.

TAMMY MALTBY
Speaker, cohost, and author of *The God Who Sees You*

The Unseen Companion is an encouraging, uplifting, heart-to-heart conversation from one single mother to another. It's a lifeline for those raising children on their own. But, more importantly, Michelle leads the single mom directly to the heart of God, where our true hope is found.

SANDY BOVÉ
Single mom of two

Michelle articulates the struggles in life, the independence we establish away from God, and she confirms the realization He is available to each of us as we release that independence to a deeper relationship. The book reveals an example of complete reliance and companionship Christ offers us. *The Unseen Companion* is insightful and rich.

TRACI HOLLINGSWORTH
Women's Ministries Coordinator, Woodmen Valley Chapel, Longmont, CO

As a publishing professional, I applaud Michelle Senters for her authentic voice and compelling personal accounts. As a single mom, I felt immense relief—she not only gets us as we are, but her insightful questions nudge us along on our faith journey.

RHONDA WRAY
Editor, Christian Publishers/Contemporary Drama Service

Reestablishing family foundations is so critical in our broken and hurting world. This book offers the "intrinsic connection" to restoration for the single mother (whether she was never married, divorced, or widowed). There is wisdom, true hope, and insightful understanding birthed from Michelle's story and her personal journey in the Word of God. Help and hope are available in *The Unseen Companion*.

STEVE AND LYNN BROWN
Faithful servants to hurting families (especially women and their children) for over thirty years

GOD *with*
THE SINGLE
MOTHER

the UNSEEN COMPANION

MICHELLE LYNN SENTERS

MOODY PUBLISHERS

CHICAGO

Edited by Elizabeth Cody Newenhuyse
Cover and interior design: Erik M. Peterson
Cover photo of geraniums copyright © 2016 by Suzanne Cummings/
        Getty Images (180472241). All rights reserved.
Author photo: Kristen Cook Evensen

Library of Congress Cataloging-in-Publication Data
Names: Senters, Michelle Lynn, author.
Title: The unseen companion : God with the single mother / Michelle Lynn
    Senters.
Description: Chicago, IL : Moody Publishers, [2017]
Identifiers: LCCN 2016050200 (print) | LCCN 2016057739 (ebook) |
    ISBN 9780802414335 | ISBN 9780802493910
Subjects: LCSH: Single mothers--Religious life.
Classification: LCC BV4529.18 .S46 2017 (print) | LCC BV4529.18 (ebook) | DDC
    248.8/431--dc23
LC record available at https://lccn.loc.gov/2016050200

We hope you enjoy this book from Moody Publishers. Our goal is to provide high-quality, thought-provoking books and products that connect truth to your real needs and challenges. For more information on other books and products written and produced from a biblical perspective, go to www.moodypublishers.com or write to:

Moody Publishers
820 N. La Salle Boulevard
Chicago, IL 60610

1 3 5 7 9 10 8 6 4 2

Printed in the United States of America

For my daughters,
Gabrielle, Rachel, and Lacey.
Thank you for encouraging me to share our story.
Just as I know the Lord as my Unseen Companion,
I pray you might always know Him as your Unseen Father.
"You are sealed with God's love and mine."
(You know the routine.)

And for single mothers,
each and every one of you.
You are not alone.

Contents

FOREWORD

In 1998, I was a struggling single mom, trying to navigate life in the midst of unbearable loneliness, fear, and exhaustion. It was a brutal year. My fiancé had recently died in an accident, and his loss was more than my fragile heart could bear. One wintry morning, while tiredly trying to unbury my car from twelve inches of freshly fallen snow, I completely came un-glued. In a fit of desperation, I lifted my shovel to the heavens, shaking it wildly while shouting, *"God, where are YOU?"*

Oh, how I wish I'd had *The Unseen Companion* back then. When I read Michelle's frequent prayer —*"God, where ARE You in this? Why won't You help me?"*—I knew she truly under-stood the demands and desperation of parenting solo. Real, engaging, and truth-filled, Michelle isn't afraid to share her struggles with authenticity and vulnerability. Yet in the midst of the stresses of single motherhood, Michelle's story perme-ates the reader with hope, peace, and strength. She demon-strates in practical ways how to reject the empty promises of the world while pursuing the love and stability found in Christ. I finished *The Unseen Companion* reminded afresh that

"God loves you. He is always with you. You are not alone."

Back to that distressing, snow-covered day in 1998. Not long after I shook my shovel in despair, a car pulled up in front of my house, and a college kid hopped out. "Hey lady," he shouted, "this looks like a pretty big driveway. Go on in the house. Let me shovel for you." Tears streamed as I tried to mutter the words, "Thank you, thank you, thank you."

The next time life circumstances cause you to wonder "*God, where are You?*," go ahead and ask Him. He might be closer than you think.

CINDY BULTEMA
Bible teacher, speaker and author of *Red Hot Faith* and *Live Full, Walk Free: Set Apart in a Sin-Soaked World*

YOU ARE NOT ALONE

You probably don't have time to read this book, and, quite honestly, I struggle to find time to write it. I look beyond the computer screen and notice the baskets of dirty laundry. Bills lie unopened on the desk. The dog needs brushing. The lawn needs water. The children need breakfast, and the outdated exercise machine calls to me with a promised loss of two dress sizes, hopefully, three. As a former single mother of eight years, *I get it*. There is little time to do the things you must, much less the things that might nurture and feed your soul. But you, my new friend, are worth nurturing.

There is a simple truth that becomes lost in the shuffle of daily life.

Lost beneath the endless to-do list.

Lost behind the sound of children's voices.

Lost within the darkness that pervades the soul in the depth of the night.

You are not alone.

"I will never leave you nor forsake you."
JOSHUA 1:5

You may feel alone. You may feel abandoned, overwhelmed, and ill-equipped for the life of a single mother, but you are not alone on this journey. The Unseen Companion is with you, even now as you hold this book in your hands. He has not forgotten or abandoned you, nor is He waiting for you to get it all together. He is *with you*. He hears every cry and whispered prayer. He watches over you and your children, and if you are willing, this Unseen Companion will help you build a strong home for your family.

Take a deep breath and let this truth settle within your heart. *You are not alone.*

Oh, and in case you've forgotten, dear single momma, *He loves you.*

"Be strong and courageous.
Do not be afraid; do not be discouraged,
for the LORD your God will be with you wherever you go."
JOSHUA 1:9

PART ONE

the
LONGING
for HOME

As I write, I can't help but wonder where you are. Perhaps you are standing in a bookstore, thumbing through this chapter and wondering if this book is for you. Maybe you found a few moments to read during your lunch break at work. But most likely, you are at home. Your children are in bed and you've finally settled down in your favorite chair for a little time to yourself. You are all warm. Safe and sound. This is where I imagine you.

May I ask you a personal question? When you are at your house, do you feel *at home*? In other words, in your quietest moments, do you feel content and secure with who and where you are in this world? When you come home from work each day, do you breathe in a sigh of relief, knowing you are where you belong? Or are you still waiting for an arrival of some sort? If you are like me, the concept of "feeling at home" seems elusive and somewhat dreamy—almost as if I have something yet to attain or find or create. While I find some sense of comfort and identity in my rented house, my heart desires something more.

Woven within the fabric of our being is a God-given longing for home. We yearn not only for a bit of land, four walls, and a roof—but *a home*. A place of refuge, safety, love, and belonging. Permanence and peace.

I remember myself as a child, scouring the neighborhood alleys, dumpsters, and fields for broken and discarded pieces of plywood and two-by-fours. I collected as much as my skinny arms could carry home. Then, equipped with a large rock and a coffee can filled with rusty nails, I began to hammer. I was a builder of forts. Wooden forts. Snow forts. Inside-the-house, blanket forts. With unrelenting determination, I built little homes for myself—personal shelters against the storms of childhood, namely my annoying little brother and sister. And once inside, I dreamed about a life of *my* choosing.

But in all those years of building and dreaming, I never envisioned *this* life. A life scattered across six states, fourteen cities, and thirty-three houses. A life stained by emotional abuse, addiction, stalking, and divorce. At thirty-two years old, I found myself standing in a desert wasteland, desperately longing for a *home*. With my young daughters clinging to the hem of my skirt, I picked up that old rock and can of rusty nails to build once again from what was broken and discarded.

Remnants of shattered dreams.

Fractured plans. Misplaced hope.

Pounded together with inadequate strength.

And that is where *He* answered my cry.

Jesus took the rock and nails from my hands and reminded me that He was a *Carpenter.*

With a steady hand and certain eyes, He lifted my family out of ruins and placed us on a firm foundation. He built a strong frame and surrounded us with protective walls. He placed a secure roof over our heads and adorned our new home with things of beauty.

Of *this* home and Builder, I write.

Unless the LORD builds the house, the builders labor in vain.
PSALM 127:1

CHAPTER 1

A BROKEN TENT

My tent is destroyed; all its ropes are snapped.
JEREMIAH 10:20

I felt tempted to yell out in frustration. Scream. Indulge myself in a well-deserved, single-momma, losing-it moment. Instead, I uttered a familiar prayer as I struck the mallet against the tent stake. *"God, where ARE you in this? Why won't you help me?"* The ground beneath, composed of broken granite and hardened dirt, refused to give way. It was my first camping trip as a single mother, and I was failing within the first twenty minutes.

My failure was not for lack of planning. Having grown up in the Wyoming mountains, I considered myself a seasoned camper. I saved for months and purchased the needed supplies. Tent. Sleeping bags. Lantern. First aid kit. Abundant "just-in-case" items. Propane stove. A campfire menu that could rival that of a five-star restaurant and peanut butter in a tube, in the event the girls didn't enjoy my outdoor culinary stylings. Neighboring campers likely assumed we intended to stay the entire summer as they watched us unload the car.

Too proud to ask for help, I continued to pound the stubborn earth with all the self-sufficient, bold-determination I could muster. I grunted and huffed. Muttered and grimaced. I may have cussed and cried a few tears, but the dry wind swept them away before anyone noticed. Forty minutes, five bent tent stakes, and three bloodied knuckles later, the tent was up, and we were finally ready for our camping adventure.

I stepped back and admired my work. The tent stood strong, and the girls raced inside with sleeping bags and pillows to claim their territory. But just as every grand adventure requires not one, but many obstacles to overcome, we were just beginning.

The rocky campsite, booked online, was situated near a busy mountain road, popular with both tourists and truckers, whose down-shifting diesel engines echoed mercilessly against the canyon walls.

Our faithful German shepherd protected us with fits of barking, lunging, and pouncing. Squirrels. Cars. People. Ladybugs clinging to milkweed. Leaves blowing in the wind. Each threat received the proper attention and decibel level it undoubtedly deserved.

The lakeshore swimming beach didn't allow pets, forcing us to carry our picnic lunch and armfuls of "just-in-case" supplies along the rocky shoreline until we reached a dog-friendly, but not-so-swimmable, area to spend the afternoon.

And once we returned to camp, the wind grew stronger, carrying more pollen than my thirteen-year-old daughter, Rachel, could withstand. She then succumbed to a three-hour nap after I inadvertently gave her too much allergy medicine.

Yes. It was a humbling kind of adventure.

Thankfully, the wind died down long enough for this

camera-toting momma to build a campfire and snap a few pictures of the girls roasting marshmallows. I watched them laugh and dance as the sun set in blazing glory behind the mountains and realized they were oblivious to my struggle. They created joyful memories despite my perceived failings and invited me to join the celebration. Gabrielle offered the gift of a s'more, with charred marshmallow and chocolate dripping between her six-year-old fingers, and for one blessed moment, my worries and failures melted into sweet goodness and little-girl giggles.

I went to bed with a full heart that evening, understanding the importance of what I accomplished. The girls snuggled deep within their sleeping bags, their eyes heavy from swimming and campfire smoke. Our dog settled down, her breathing slow and restful. All was quiet and good, except for the wind. And traffic. And neighboring campers, but I didn't mind. I prevailed despite the circumstances and, somehow, that gave me assurance that I could tackle this single-momma thing. If I could muscle tent stakes into rocky ground, perhaps I could attempt grander things. *Maybe I could save enough money to buy a little camping trailer. We could fix it up retro style and visit all the national parks . . .*

I fell asleep feeling courageous and self-reliant, unaware of the increasing wind and impending storm.

> *"The rain came down, the streams rose,*
> *and the winds blew and beat against that house,*
> *and it fell with a great crash."*
> **MATTHEW 7:27**

The sun burned hot against the tent the next morning, and before I opened my eyes, I lingered in dreams of howling wind and breaking branches. The sound of a speedboat in the distance startled me awake and into the awareness that I had not been dreaming. While we slept through the night, the wind broke our tent, snapping several poles in two and collapsing a wall on one side. The girls woke up disoriented and upset, tearfully assuming it was time to pack up and go home.

But I, both creative and stubborn, refused to disappoint my daughters. As I cooked them pancakes and bacon over the camp stove, I remembered the ingenuity of my fort-making days and made a mental list of repair supplies. Duct tape. Knife. Long sticks for support. *Tree branches, perhaps?* Rope. *This could work. It had to.*

While I gathered supplies, a fellow single mother arrived with her daughter, as planned months earlier. We surveyed the damage together and realized it was much worse than originally thought. The morning wind blew the rain cover away, and the tent was almost entirely collapsed now. My friend forced a smile and indulged me a few moments of shameless naïveté and unabashed optimism as I informed her of my repair plans.

"Michelle," she began.

That's all it took. I looked away, feeling the familiar sense of failure rise in my throat.

"It's over," she said. "You can't fix this. Sometimes it's okay to give up."

You don't understand. We need this. I need this, I protested in silence, staring at the insurmountable mountain before me and desperately wanting to move it by sheer force of will.

My friend took my hand in hers. "It's time for you to go home."

And while our girls played safely in the distance, I had that well-deserved, single-momma, losing-it moment beside my dear friend. We both knew I would return to a home just as broken as my tent.

A Season of List-Making

I left the campground that afternoon with one goal in mind. I intended to fix everything broken in our life, starting with that pathetic tent. The next morning, a grinning salesman at the sporting goods store listened as I voiced my complaint. He winked at the girls and agreed that a single mom and her children should have a safe and reliable tent for their camping adventures. I couldn't tell if he found amusement in our camping disaster or if he felt genuine concern, but we walked out of the store with a new tent, guaranteed to shelter us from the fiercest of Colorado winds. No extra charge.

1. ~~Return broken tent.~~ *Done.*

And that marked the beginning of my list-making season. I wrote down every failure, every frustration, every task I need to accomplish to "fix" our broken home.

2. Clean the house and keep it clean.
3. Decorate. Make this rental a *home*.
4. Play with the girls more often. Have fun. Go on adventures and vacations.
5. Create chore lists, discipline plans, and homework schedules that work.
6. Deal with finances.
7. Hire attorney to pursue child support. *(Make more money so I can afford an attorney.)*
8. Go back to college.
9. Exercise. Eat right. Lose weight.

10. Pursue emotional healing for the girls and me. Go to a counselor.
11. Go back to church.
12. Find a husband to love us and complete our family.

Empowered by my "to-do" list, complete with the perceived "I've arrived" goal of getting married, I picked up that old rock and can of rusty nails and attempted to build a new life and home for my daughters. Over the next several years, I carefully budgeted my teaching salary. I read self-help books and cleaned out my closets. I took out student loans and returned to school during the weekends, eventually earning a master's degree in education. I set healthy boundaries and household rules. I mowed the lawn, pulled weeds, and planted flowers. I went on bad dates. Terrible dates. *What was I thinking? Is he seriously snoring through the movie?* kind of dates.

Now, it might seem as if I was quite productive in crossing items off my list, and perhaps you've attempted to rebuild your home with the same tenacity. If so, you probably felt like I did. For every brick I laid, another three fell. I simply couldn't build a home that could stand.

Friends offered consoling hugs and well-meaning words of encouragement. "All you need is God." "Don't worry; God is with you." "All things happen for a reason." "You're the toughest woman I know." And my least favorite, "God isn't going to give you anything you can't handle."

Oh, really? Well, God must think I'm Wonder Woman.

I kept my snarky attitude to myself. My friends spoke with sincerity, and I embraced their concern, but the overused platitudes did little for my single-momma heart. I soon grew skeptical of hope professed by those who lived a life markedly different from my own. Few understood the grave reality of my situation. I was economically ruined. Sexually vulnerable. Overwhelmed. Lonely. Wounded. Physically and emotionally spent. I needed tangible help, and the world stood before me with arms open wide, offering the practical "solutions" to which any single mother could fall prey: relationships, distractions, lists, and "void fillers."

"Are you lonely? Join this website. I have men lined up, waiting to meet you."

"Is life more than you can bear? I have pleasurable distractions to take your mind off things. Grab a glass of wine at 2 a.m. and watch this movie. You will feel much better about yourself."

"Are you tired? This energy supplement will enable you to climb the highest mountain."

"Is your life a mess? Follow my easy, fail-proof, ten-step plan to a better life. Only $39.95, if you call in the next ten minutes."

And so, with a "to-do" list clutched in my fist, I fell into the arms and empty promises of the world, believing they would eventually provide the home and security I longed for.

> *"What they trust in is fragile;*
> *what they rely on is a spider's web.*
> *They lean on the web, but it gives way;*
> *they cling to it, but it does not hold."*
> **JOB 8:14–15**

But no matter how many books I read—no matter how many nails I pounded—our ramshackle house continued to fall. The lists lengthened. The debt grew. My loneliness increased, and the girls struggled under the weight of brokenness. While continuing my education was honorable and set a good example for my daughters, it did not fill my heart's longing. It did not solve any problems or make life as a single mother easier. Nor did relationships, distractions, or a clean house. They may have offered a temporary delight and satisfaction, but eventually they revealed themselves for what they truly were: counterfeit hope and short-lived joy.

Our home was in shambles, and although I didn't realize it at the time, I was faced with two choices. I could either continue building on broken ground, or I could ask God to rebuild my home.

I chose the latter.

"In that day I will restore David's fallen shelter —
I will repair its broken walls and restore its ruins —
and will rebuild it as it used to be . . ."
AMOS 9:11

HOMEBUILDING 101:
The Longing for Home

A Broken Tent

BUILDING YOUR HOME:

Consider the following areas of need for single mothers: balance, companionship, provision, healing, rest, strength, protection, peace, love, and identity.

1. How are you doing in each of these areas? In which areas do you need help or healing?

2. In your areas of greatest need, what temptations and false promises does the world offer you?

3. In which areas do you feel God's presence and blessing?

Review the Scriptures below. Both the prophet Amos and King David emphasized that it is only the Lord who builds a home with strength and sustenance.

> *In that day I will restore David's fallen shelter—*
> *I will repair its broken walls and restore its ruins—*
> *and will rebuild it as it used to be . . .*
>
> **AMOS 9:11**

Unless the LORD builds the house, the builders labor in vain.
PSALM 127:1

4. Do you define your home as "broken"?
5. How do these Scriptures speak to you as a single mother?
6. In your prayers, speak to God about the "condition" of your home, and ask Him to help you restore the areas of brokenness.

BUILDING A LEGACY OF FAITH:
At the end of each chapter, I will share ideas to help you build a strong and lasting legacy of faith in your children. These easy and practical suggestions will empower you to apply the truths found in each chapter as you parent your children.

PRAY FOR AND WITH YOUR CHILD
After nearly twenty-three years of parenting, I'm still learning the remarkable power that prayer has in the lives of my children. Praying *for* your children will strengthen and support the years of love, discipline, and wisdom you've invested because it evokes the hand of God to act on behalf of your family. Prayer is not a last-resort effort if all else fails. It is not second-best. Rather, prayer invites God into your family as the Father and Head of your household. You are no longer alone in your parenting, as prayer acts as a conduit of wisdom and strength between you and God.

In addition, praying *with* your children is one of the most powerful ways you can help your child develop a *relationship* with God.

Rejoice always, pray continually, give thanks in all circumstances; for this is God's will for you in Christ Jesus.
1 THESSALONIANS 5:16–18

But teaching your child to pray can be an intimidating task if you are uncomfortable or inexperienced with praying aloud. Begin by praying with your child before bed. Your prayer does not need to be long or eloquent. Simply "talk" to God. My daughters and I called these "heartfelt prayers." After hearing your prayers for a time, ask your children if there is anything they would like to say to God. In time, your children will feel comfortable praying aloud.

If you prefer a format, Jesus modeled the now-beloved "Lord's Prayer" in Matthew 6:9–13, or you can use the ACTS method of prayer, which includes:

A—Adoration (Worship and praise God for who He is. Name His attributes and character.)

C—Confession (Confess your sins and ask God for forgiveness.)

T—Thanksgiving (Thank God for the blessings of this life.)

S—Supplication (Make specific requests of God.)

Example of an ACTS prayer offered by the mother of a school-age child:

Dear God, When I think about the world and all You have created, I am in awe of who You are. Please forgive me for losing my patience today. I was wrong to yell without understanding the whole situation first. Thank You for loving me and forgiving me. Thank You for my family and all You have given us. Please be with us tomorrow as we travel to Grandma's house. Keep us safe and help us to shine our light, wherever we go. Amen.

Example of an ACTS prayer by a school-age child:

Dear God, You are strong, and You are good. You created the whole world, and You created me. Please forgive me for yelling at my sister. Thank You for loving me and my family. Please help us to be nice to each other. Amen.

For older children who may feel resistant to prayer, begin by telling them on occasion that you are praying for them. In time, share a little about what you are praying for or what God may be telling you. Share a Scripture that you pray over them. Eventually, you may have the opportunity to respond to a situation by asking your child if you can pray over them in that moment. For children who are resistant to prayer, Scripture, or believing in God, it is crucial to ask for God's wisdom on how to proceed. It is very easy for a child to misconstrue genuine prayer as a form of manipulation.

Start children off on the way they should go, and even when they are old they will not turn from it.
—PROVERBS 22:6

CHAPTER 2

A THIRST for SOMETHING MORE

My soul thirsts for God, for the living God.
When can I go and meet with God?

PSALM 42:2

Single mothers, do you know I pray for you?

Even now, my stitched-up heart splits open once again as I recall my journey and consider the weight of responsibility and worry you now carry. How I long to cry out to you with the blessed assurance of God's love and provision, "God IS enough! Trust in Him! Let go of the things of this world, and run to Him who loves you!"

But, it's not that easy, is it? Such assurances seem like cruel fairytales in the midst of legitimate need and pain. *Don't speak to me about the love of God when I am busy sweeping up the shattered remains of my life.*

Although I remarried six years ago, your struggle is not lost on me. The voice of the single mother—your voice—long remains my language of fluency. I remember well the questions, doubt, and cynicism that grew within me, threatening all I once knew about God.

I believed in God's existence and understood my salvation came through the death of Jesus on the cross. Even as a child, faith helped me to withstand my parents' divorce and the inevitable consequences of brokenness. When my brother, sister, and I visited our father during the summers, I held secret church services for the three of us, complete with traditional liturgy, candles, and flattened Wonder Bread for communion.

Belief was never the issue. *Relationship* was.

As the stories of my life unfolded through adulthood, leaving me, at times, in immediate danger and desperate need, I seriously doubted God's *presence* in my life. His *interest*. I knew God loved others, but secretly questioned His love for *me*. If God was all-knowing and all-powerful—if His love for me was all-consuming—why didn't He simply fix the issues I was powerless to control?

I couldn't protect my oldest daughter from self-harm.

I couldn't entice a man to fall in love with me.

I couldn't make enough money to pay the bills or miraculously make child support checks appear.

I couldn't even afford a babysitter so that I could have time to myself.

But God *could* and chose not to. I didn't know what to do with that. Couldn't the Creator, who put the stars in their places and set the earth to spin, also create something of worth and beauty in me? Couldn't the same hand that calmed the storm remove the raging torrents in my life? Jesus multiplied the loaves of bread and fish to feed the masses. Could He not multiply what little I had? While God obviously blessed countless families around me, it seemed He removed His hand from mine.

> *"Do you have only one blessing, my father?*
> *Bless me too, my father!" Then Esau wept aloud.*
> **GENESIS 27:38**

It is within our human nature to long for our father's blessing. In Genesis, Jacob fooled his blind and aging father into bestowing on him the blessing that rightfully belonged to his older brother Esau. We feel Esau's stark sorrow as he begs his father for a blessing. "Then Esau wept aloud."

The word for "wept" in the original Hebrew text is *bakah*, which means to bewail with great disappointment, grief, or bitterness. It is the kind of mourning that causes one to clutch their chest and fall to the ground in writhing pain. Just as Esau wept in anguish over his stolen blessing and birthright, I wept at the loss of my childhood dreams. I hadn't asked for much, only that which seemed a rightful inheritance for every woman. A loving husband. Happy children. A little house of our own. I lost what little I asked for, and adding grief upon grief, I believed I was entirely alone in my journey as a single mother.

I felt forsaken by God and man and society. Forgotten. Cut off and abandoned. Like David in the Psalms, my prayers were reduced to exhausted one-liners. *God, where ARE YOU in this? Why won't you help me? Do you even see me? Hear me?*

> *My God, my God, why have you forsaken me?*
> *Why are you so far from saving me,*
> *so far from my cries of anguish?*
> *My God, I cry out by day, but you do not answer,*
> *by night, but I find no rest.*
> **PSALM 22:1-2**

Yet, even in my anger and disillusionment, I considered myself a Christian. *I loved God*, but quite honestly, I did not *know* Him. I knew *of* Him. And because I was largely unfamiliar with the Bible, I based my understanding of God solely on the logic of this world.

I presumed God shared the world's attitude toward single mothers, especially those who were single mothers by divorce. "You got yourself into this, so deal with it." "God gave you a brain. He expects you to use it to solve your problems." The world told me I was a weight and burden to society, and, as a result, I felt hesitant to ask anything of God. The world devalued my thoughts and contributions, leading me to believe I had nothing to offer Him. Married women looked at me with suspicion and at my children with pity. Men regarded me as either an object of desire or disdain. Even my church, with its four walls, cross, and intact families, became a house of mirrors, reflecting all I had once aspired to and failed to become. It was logical to assume I had moved far beyond God's reach and concern.

The inherent problem with this world-based theology is its inability to grasp the unmerited grace and love of Jesus.

> *I do not give to you as the world gives.*
> **JOHN 14:27**

I had no interest in a book about God's love for *other* people. I wanted another SELF-help book with a new-and-improved, easy-to-follow, ten-step-plan to become a better single mother. I wanted a list of rules. A regimen. A cure. In an act of sheer desperation, I reached instead for the last dusty book on my shelf.

My Bible.

Perhaps it contained the list I needed to earn God's blessing once again.

HOPE FOUND ME AT THE WELL

"I have food to eat that you know nothing about."
JOHN 4:32

Have you ever had a moment in which you are reading a book and find yourself so immersed within the story that it becomes less about the character and more about you? A story so profound it reaches the darkened chambers of your inner being, revealing what you had always known or longed for, but never had the courage to put into words?

The Gospel of John, chapter 4, offered such a moment for me and continues to serve as an important mile-marker in my journey as a single mother. At first read, the story of the "Woman at the Well" simply appeared to be an account in which Jesus revealed Himself as the Messiah. And as usual, Jesus spoke in confounding metaphors, offering "living water" to the woman and telling His disciples He had "food" they knew nothing about. But how did that relate to me as a single mother in the twenty-first century? While the woman had been married five times and was living with a sixth man, it wasn't clear if she was even a mother.

As I read through the pages of her story a second and third time, I came to a humbling realization. I was *also* a woman at the well, dipping my bucket into the deep earth, hoping to draw out something to quench my thirsty soul. And Jesus was waiting there to give me His living water. *Oh, please, Lord, give me something to ease this thirst!*

That is the brilliance and beauty of the Bible. The authors provide enough information to help us picture ourselves within God's story, yet graciously omit details that may disqualify our connection. Her story, therefore, becomes my story. And yours.

Take a few minutes now to reacquaint yourself with the woman at the well. Read John 4:1–42, and imagine yourself in her place. How would you feel? What would your impression be of this man named Jesus?

Her story moves us beyond the world-based theology of condemnation and shame by teaching us two paradigm-shifting lessons:

1. Jesus deals tenderly with women in difficult circumstances. Being fully God, nothing remains hidden from Jesus. She was a Samaritan woman, considered unclean and beyond God's redemption—not only because of the race she was born into, but also in the sin that ostracized her from her community. Jesus knew the intimate details of her life, and yet He did not condemn her, nor did He shame or ridicule. Instead, He spoke gentle words of truth, revealing His full knowledge of her, and offered the gift of living water, a lasting refreshment for her soul.

> *"If you knew the gift of God and who it is*
> *that asks you for a drink,*
> *you would have asked him and he would have*
> *given you living water."*
> **JOHN 4:10**

Even more remarkable was the fact Jesus chose *this woman* as the *first* to know His identity as the Messiah. Jesus could have revealed Himself as the Messiah to the religious teachers and political leaders of the land. He could have announced it from a mountaintop, garnering thousands of worshipers at His feet. Instead, He chose a woman of little significance.

> *The woman said, "I know that Messiah"*
> *(called Christ) "is coming.*
> *When he comes, he will explain everything to us."*
> *Then Jesus declared, "I, the one speaking to you—I am he."*
> **JOHN 4:25-26**

Jesus not only knew her, but He also allowed Himself to be known.

This is the same Jesus who prevented an adulterous woman from being stoned to death. The Jesus who allowed a sinful woman to wash His feet with tears and anoint Him with perfume. He healed the woman with an issue of blood and another with a bent back. He spoke with fondness about the poor widow who gave all she had to the temple treasury, and He praised Mary, who willingly set aside the important work of the day to sit at His feet and learn from Him. And after Jesus rose from the grave, He appeared first to the grieving Mary Magdalene, a woman from whom He cast out seven demons. Yes, our Savior has a tender heart toward women in difficult circumstances.

If He knew the real me and all that I've done, surely He would reject me. If He knew the intensity of my anger and my irresponsibility with money. If He knew the abuse I endured and my inability to stop it. If He saw the difficulty I have raising my children on my own and the hopelessness and resentment I carry. If He really knew me . . .

Rest assured, single mother. He knows you fully, even the doubts and cynicism you wrestle with in this moment. He waits for you at the well, not with condemnation, but with living water and the invitation to know Him.

2. Jesus offers living water to quench our souls. As the woman walked to the well that morning, she never could have anticipated the remarkable event that was to take place. She intended to fill her vessel with water and left instead with a heart filled with grace and truth.

Like the woman at the well, we are thirsty women. We thirst not only for the basic necessities of this life, but also for companionship, love, security, and peace. We thirst for strength, healing, and significance. And when our thirst becomes unbearable, we walk to the wells of this world in hopes of filling our vessels with something that will support and sustain us.

Jesus made a stunning claim.

"Everyone who drinks this water will be thirsty again, but whoever drinks the water I give them will never thirst. Indeed, the water I give them will become in them a spring of water welling up to eternal life."
JOHN 4:13-14

While Jesus understood the woman would return to the well for water to sustain her physical body, He offered living water to sustain her soul.

I know what you may be thinking. *Living water sounds great in theory, but I'm struggling to pay rent and put food on the table. I have to live in reality. Give me something practical.*

I get it. Remember, I was that list-making single momma who ran into the open arms and empty promises of this world. I drank from the wells and stagnant cisterns, yet I remained thirsty.

Eternally thirsty.

While our bodies thirst for water, our souls thirst for what is eternal.

> *You, God, are my God, earnestly I seek you;*
> *I thirst for you, my whole being longs for you,*
> *in a dry and parched land where there is no water.*
> **PSALM 63:1**

We live in a broken world, dear one. Being a Christian does not ensure a life free from suffering and pain, nor are we promised a life free from want. But through His living water, God empowers us to walk through difficult circumstances with courage, dignity, and grace. And for those of us who need to rebuild our homes, God's Word shows the intrinsic connection between living water and restoration.

> *The LORD will guide you always;*
> *he will satisfy your needs in a sun-scorched land*
> *and will strengthen your frame.*
> *You will be like a well-watered garden,*
> *like a spring whose waters never fail.*
> *Your people will rebuild the ancient ruins*
> *and will raise up the age-old foundations;*
> *you will be called Repairer of Broken Walls,*
> *Restorer of Streets with Dwellings.*
> **ISAIAH 58:11–12**

Did you *see* that? The Old Testament prophet Isaiah, the same man who prophesied Jesus' birth, says we will be called "Repairer of Broken Walls" and "Restorer of Streets with Dwellings." Through His living water, God strengthens us to raise up our foundations and repair our broken walls. What a comforting promise for those of us who define our homes as broken.

RETURNING TO MY PEOPLE

Over the years, many have questioned why I continue in ministry to single mothers, long after I remarried. "Don't you want to forget about that time and move on?" they ask. I smile and recall the woman at the well. After Jesus had revealed Himself as the Messiah, the woman returned to her people in the village. She shared her testimony, and as a result, many people came to believe in Jesus.

Then, leaving her water jar, the woman went back to the town and said to the people,
"Come, see a man who told me everything I ever did.
Could this be the Messiah?"
JOHN 4:28-29

Single mothers, *YOU* are my village. The people I love and whose stories are similar to my own. I return to share the good news with you. "I've seen the Messiah! He knows everything we've ever done and yet He still loves us. He's come to bind up our broken hearts and heal our wounds. He will rebuild our homes and carry our children on His arm. Trust in Him. Let go of the things of this world and run to Him who loves you. He will give you living water!"

These assurances are not the words of a cruel fairytale. Rather, they are words of truth, spoken from one who's been there.

He *is* enough.

Jesus stood and said in a loud voice,
"Let anyone who is thirsty come to me and drink.
Whoever believes in me, as Scripture has said,
rivers of living water will flow from within them."
JOHN 7:37-38

HOMEBUILDING 101:
The Longing for Home

A Thirst for Something More

BUILDING YOUR HOME:

Think about the story of the "Woman at the Well" from John 4:1–42.

1. Do you identify with the woman at the well and if so, how?

2. What do you thirst for most in this life?

3. Do you believe that God can satisfy your needs and longings? Why or why not?

4. In your prayers, ask God for the living water promised to the woman at the well.

BUILDING A LEGACY OF FAITH: Bless your child

Earlier in the chapter, we remembered Esau's anguish over his stolen blessing and birthright. "'Do you have only one blessing, my father? Bless me too, my father!' Then Esau wept aloud" (Gen. 27:38). Today's research indicates that the perceived lack of parental blessing and acceptance in children often leads to devastating consequences lasting a lifetime. Conversely, children who receive verbal and physical blessings from at least one parent tend to show more signs of stability, contentment, and openness to a relationship with God.

Long before I was a single mother, I took the advice of my pastor and blessed my children each night through words and touch. As I tucked my daughters into bed, I traced a cross on their forehead and said, "You are sealed with God's love and mine." Then I kissed their forehead. This simple routine—played out thousands of times—helped my children to feel secure and safe, even in the most difficult of circumstances.

> *He anointed us, set his seal of ownership on us,*
> *and put his Spirit in our hearts as a deposit,*
> *guaranteeing what is to come.*
> **2 CORINTHIANS 1:21–22**

Create a simple bedtime blessing that includes both words and touch, or use the example shown above. This small act will create a lasting tradition that will continue into the next generation.

For older children who may feel resistant to a "bedtime ritual," speak words of blessing over them from time to time during the day. Touch their shoulder or arm momentarily, and look your children in the eye. Speak about their God-given talents and your vision for a positive future. Offer words of hope, encouragement, and grace. Remind them of your love and God's love.

Some examples of blessings may include:

"Wow. When I consider the gifts and abilities God has given you, I can't help but see amazing things in your future."

"I believe God will do a great work in your life someday."

"I know you can do this. You've worked hard and God has equipped you well."

"With God's help, I believe you can do anything you set your mind to and work hard for."

"There is nothing you can do that will separate you from God's love or mine" (during difficult times).

By including the power, provision, and hand of God in these phrases, we teach our children that God is ever present and ready to help. They are not expected to do it on their own.

PART TWO

the

FOUNDATION

*"The rain came down, the streams rose,
and the winds blew and beat against that house;
yet it did not fall, because it had its foundation on the rock."*

MATTHEW 7:25

CHAPTER 3

BALANCE

When I am overwhelmed,
He is my Rock.

*Truly he is my rock and my salvation; he is my fortress,
I will never be shaken.*

PSALM 62:2

The workshop *seemed* like a good idea, at the time. After all, I was still in my list-making season, carefully planning goals that I might someday achieve success as a single mother. The problem did not lie in an inability to *set* goals. I was quite adept at identifying objectives and the steps required to achieve them. The problem lay in my inability to *work toward* my goals. The responsibilities of day-to-day life overwhelmed me, and, as a result, there remained little time and energy to devote to anything beyond mere survival. Despite my struggle, I still clung to the false belief that to "BE much" in life I had to "DO much," so a workshop on balance seemed like a perfect solution.

Having struggled to get the girls to the babysitter on time, I hurriedly took my place in the crowded church auditorium with only minutes to spare. I shut my eyes and drew in a deep breath, trying to regain a sense of peace and presence. *I made it. Finally a little "me" time.* Going to a workshop was an indulgent treat, and I intended to savor every moment.

But as I fumbled in my canvas bag for a notebook and pen, I took notice of the women surrounding me and wondered if I was perhaps in the wrong place. These women were *beautiful*. Polished and professional. Hair coiffed. Nails buffed. They wore stilettos with jeans and carried their notebooks and water bottles in designer handbags. Their diamond wedding rings sparkled under the gleaming brilliance of their newly whitened teeth.

Okay. Maybe that last one was a slight exaggeration, but the difference between us was striking.

I studied my hands. They were simply the tools with which I carried out the tasks of each day. Painfully neglected. Dry. Nail-bitten. Ink-stained from hours of desperate journaling. My ring finger bore the mark of my shame. Although I had removed my wedding band years earlier, a deep indentation remained, and perhaps that was the greatest difference.

The indentation left behind.

The women chatted amongst themselves in happy unity, unaware of my observation. Actually, they were unaware of me altogether, yet I still felt compelled to uncross my legs and hide my sole-worn shoes and bag beneath my chair. A chasm stood wide and deep between us, echoing needless reminders of all I was not.

Why are these women attending a workshop on balance? They don't look overwhelmed. They apparently have enough time and money for manicures.

Once again, my snarky attitude rose to help me maintain a semblance of composure. I kept deep emotion at arm's length, especially in public places, and internal sarcasm and cynicism were among my best defensive weapons. I could not afford the luxury of a meltdown. Not here.

Soon, I immersed myself in note-taking, as we learned about prioritizing goals, saying "no," and the importance of rest. As the speaker's voice faded into a drone of predictable suggestions, I pictured myself walking a tightrope far above the stage. *While the legendary circus anthem, "Entrance of the Gladiators," pumped through the loudspeakers, I moved with poetic elegance across the rope, juggling the "stuff" of life. Work. Money. Relationships. Children. Faith. I caught each plate as it was thrown to me, and both my pride and sequined tutu sparkled in the glory of the spotlight. I juggled five plates with ease. Six plates. Seven. But as the music swelled in knowing anticipation, I faltered and lost balance.*

The audience gasped as I dangled from the tightrope with one hand, my legs flailing about in wild abandon. I watched my plates of responsibility fall, one by one, to the squeals and delight of my stilettoed spectators. And when my fingers could no longer hold the weight of failure, I let go and joined the shattered remains of my life on the stage floor. As the audience rose to their feet in a thunderous ovation, I realized I was not the beautiful tightrope walker I had imagined. I was merely the comedic relief. I swept up my mess into a dustpan, took an obligatory bow, straightened my tutu, and exited stage left.

"And now, we will take a serious look at how we are managing."

The speaker snapped me back into reality. *I know exactly how I'm managing, thank you. I'm failing, lady. Didn't you just see my plates drop?*

"In each of your packets, you will find a chart to help de-

termine how well-balanced you are. Take a few minutes to fill
it out; then we'll continue."

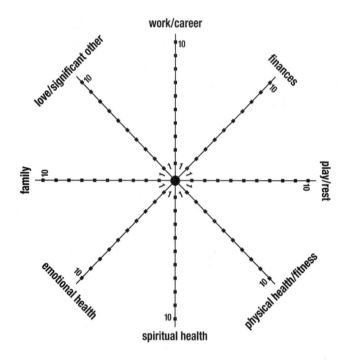

We were instructed to place a dot to represent our level
of stability and fulfillment in each area of life, with 10 repre-
senting the highest level of satisfaction; then we were to connect the dots. I generally despised "in-your-face self-analysis"
tasks, and this day proved no exception. But in my hunger for
answers, I evaluated each area with my usual abundance of
shaming self-deprecation.

"Now ladies, this is when it gets hard," the speaker continued, unaware of my desperation to slip out of the auditorium. "Imagine your chart as the tire on your proverbial wheelbarrow of life. Look at the shape."

This is supposed to look like a wheel? My eyes darted to the papers of the women who surrounded me, wondering if I had perhaps misunderstood the directions.

"How is this wheel working out for you? To live an effective, efficient, and productive life, you must allocate your time and resources EQUALLY in ALL the areas of your life. Then you will be able to push your wheelbarrow of life wherever you want it to go. THAT is balance, ladies."

While the other women chatted amongst themselves, I

slunk deeper into my seat and stared at my busted-up wheelbarrow wheel.

Well, there it was.

Proof.

It's not like I needed additional validation after my imaginary tightrope debacle. I knew I was failing, but somehow, holding the broken wheel in my hands served as a certificate of identity. *I* was a failure and, apparently, me and my wheelbarrow weren't going anywhere in life.

Later that evening, when all was quiet, and the girls had fallen asleep, I grabbed my broken wheel, unfinished to-do lists, and prayer journal and had it out with God.

Arise, cry out in the night, as the watches of the night begin;
pour out your heart like water in the presence of the Lord.
LAMENTATIONS 2:19

A JOURNAL ENTRY

Dear Lord,

This is not the life I imagined! While I once dreamed of living with passion and purpose, I now swim in the stagnant pools of mediocrity. I drown in "to-do" lists and meaningless tasks, forgetting to cherish the simple pleasure of taking my girls to the park. In my desperation to survive, I lose the joy and wonder of motherhood. And when I stand in the presence of a truly great woman as she speaks of her children, husband, and home, I smile in reply and hide my heart, pounding with shame and jealousy. In those moments of sober judgment, I am most small.

I want to run and play with my children and feel the warmth of the sun on my face, but there is too much to do and I DON'T

KNOW HOW TO DO IT ALL! Work and budget. Grocery shop, cook, and clean the house. Kill the bug. Fix the toilet. Deal with homework, bath time, and bedtime. Nurture and discipline. Play and protect. Bandage the wounds. Lock the door. Pay the bills.

Oh Lord, I can't even pay my bills.

I am overwhelmed and alone. And when I contemplate all I must do, I sit motionless, unable to accomplish even the smallest task. I am tired. Too tired to take my girls to the park.

LORD! WHERE ARE YOU IN THIS? Help me to build a life and home for my girls. I can't do this by myself.

Amen.

WORLDLY BALANCE

It appears we are not alone in our quest for balance. Just today, an Internet search for "balance in life" pulled up 368,000,000 results within 0.64 seconds. With millions of fail-proof, ten-step plans available, it is a wonder that anyone should struggle. According to the contemporary wisdom of this world, we find balance by determining our priorities, setting goals, and purposefully distributing our time, energy, and resources into the various areas of life. If we employ these habits with consistency, while always remembering to rest, the world promises a life of peace, productivity, stability, and happiness.

Whew. Sounds *easy*, doesn't it?

Now, I believe there is great wisdom found in caring for ourselves and effectively managing our time and resources. Even the smallest improvement can reap lasting rewards. For example, I felt convicted to make significant changes in my life as a single mother after completing a ten-minute exercise found in a self-help book. I simply listed my daily activities and determined if they were in alignment with my priorities and values. I was shocked to see how much time I spent in activities that were not reflective of who I was or who I wanted to become.

> *Be very careful, then, how you live—not as*
> *unwise but as wise, making the most of every*
> *opportunity, because the days are evil.*
> **EPHESIANS 5:15-16**

While this knowledge inspired me to take a thoughtful approach to how I spend my time, it did not provide the lasting stability and peace I needed. More often than not, my self-imposed, list-making, goal-setting attempts to find balance led to a predictable cycle of frustration, failure, shame, and isolation. I just couldn't keep up.

Can you relate, dear single mom? Perhaps your life looks similar to mine—a frantic juggling act of obligations, expectations, and distractions, poorly managed through an endless rotation of sticky notes and to-do lists. You might feel pressure to not only accomplish the tasks of everyday life, but also to provide your children with the same measure of love, attention, time, possessions, and lifestyle as a two-parent home. Or maybe you have grown so weary, you've long abandoned the juggling act and only have enough energy to deal with the issues immediately in front of you. And yet, there are even some who have given up completely and deliberately choose to avoid all things pertaining to responsibility. *I get it.* I've experienced each stage at one point or another.

*We were under great pressure, far beyond our ability
to endure, so that we despaired of life itself.
Indeed, we felt we had received the sentence of death.
But this happened that we might not rely on
ourselves but on God, who raises the dead.*

2 CORINTHIANS 1:8–9

With this level of responsibility and stress, is balance a realistic expectation for single mothers? *Let me sing it from the mountaintop. Yes!* Balance *is* within reach, but it might look different than you expect.

*Jesus looked at them and said, "With man this is impossible,
but with God all things are possible."*

MATTHEW 19:26

Biblical Balance

Unlike its worldly counterpart, biblical balance has nothing to do with performance or completed checklists. Biblical balance is the stability found in having our feet and home firmly planted on the rock that is Jesus Christ.

At first, I approached this truth with arms crossed, believing it was nothing more than a spiritual pacifier designed to silence the questions of struggling Christians. Because I wanted immediate, tangible, and measurable help, the concept of biblical balance quickly fell into the category of irrelevant Christianese. Nothing more.

"Just stand on the Rock. You'll be okay."

But over time, I experienced the radical transformation that occurs when the Word of God embeds itself within the heart. And as I embraced His Word as Truth, I learned three lessons, crucial to rebuilding my single parent home.

1. God lifts us and places us on high ground. We are fallible human beings. We stumble and trip. We make unwise choices and easily fall victim to circumstances beyond our control. In my inability to juggle the responsibilities and expectations of life, I cried out to God, "LORD! WHERE ARE YOU IN THIS? Please help me!" I found His answer in His Word.

I waited patiently for the LORD;
he turned to me and heard my cry.
He lifted me out of the slimy pit, out of the mud and mire;
he set my feet on a rock and gave me a firm place to stand.
PSALM 40:1-2

While thankful for God's saving hand, I quickly learned that standing on the rock did not remove the to-do lists or lessen my weight of responsibility. I woke up each morning to the same routine and pressures. But because God lifted me to a higher place, my perspective changed, enabling me to view my life differently and come up with reasonable strategies that I would have otherwise never known. Having a different vantage point also made it abundantly clear what obstructions needed to be removed from my life.

2. A house built on the rock withstands storms. When we build our house on the unpredictable and uncontrollable things of this world, the smallest amount of hardship threatens our home's structural integrity and our personal stability. Anchoring our home to the rock, however, provides an immovable foundation, allowing us to face life's inevitable storms with courage, perseverance, and hope. Instead of feeling thrown about by every wind and gale, I felt sheltered, knowing our home was a safe refuge.

> *We are hard pressed on every side, but not crushed;*
> *perplexed, but not in despair; persecuted, but not abandoned;*
> *struck down, but not destroyed.*
> **2 CORINTHIANS 4:8-9**

> *"Therefore everyone who hears these words of mine*
> *and puts them into practice is like a wise man*
> *who built his house on the rock.*
> *The rain came down, the streams rose, and the winds*
> *blew and beat against that house; yet it did not fall,*
> *because it had its foundation on the rock.*
> *But everyone who hears these words of mine and*
> *does not put them into practice is like a foolish man*
> *who built his house on sand.*
> *The rain came down, the streams rose, and the winds blew*
> *and beat against that house, and it fell with a great crash."*
> **MATTHEW 7:24-27**

3. Jesus serves as our foundation and chief cornerstone. As our foundation, Jesus gives enduring strength and stability to our home. As the chief cornerstone, He provides the perfect standard from which the entire structure is measured and built. Jesus not only supports us, He shows the way through His words and teaching.

But each one should build with care.
For no one can lay any foundation other than the
one already laid, which is Jesus Christ.
1 CORINTHIANS 3:10-11

. . . with Christ Jesus himself as the chief cornerstone.
In him the whole building is joined together and rises to
become a holy temple in the Lord.
EPHESIANS 2:20-21

A Bit of Truth and Grace

Single moms, I encourage you to lay it all down before God, right now—the to-do lists, the impossible demands, the unrealistic expectations, the broken wheelbarrow wheels, and the shame in not being able to do it all. Release it to His care, if only for a moment, and take a deep breath.

May I offer you the bit of truth and grace I desperately needed years ago?

God does not require you to keep everything under perfect control. He does not keep a list of failures, and He does not judge you by the standards of the world.

"As the heavens are higher than the earth,
so are my ways higher than your ways
and my thoughts than your thoughts."
ISAIAH 55:9

Your identity and stability are not determined by your performance. You are not a juggling tightrope walker. Nor are you the juggling, tightrope walking, comedic relief. In fact, God didn't place that tightrope in front of you. It is self-imposed, which means you have the ability to get off of it and get rid of it. And it's time to burn the tutu, no matter how sparkly it is. If you expect yourself to be Superwoman, burn the cape.

I write in all seriousness, friend.

It's time to abandon this false belief system about balance. Improving your life management skills shows wisdom, so go to workshops. Write your goals. Dream big dreams. Determine your priorities and take care of your body. But, do not trust, even for a moment, that your ability to achieve a high level of balance will provide you with a strong foundation. It is as stable as trying to build your home on a galvanized steel tightrope, two inches in diameter, suspended twenty feet off the ground.

God has entrusted you with an important job during this season of being a single mother. You are a *co-builder with God* and together you will restore your home and establish a new legacy for your children. In your longing for balance and stability, build your home on the rock that is Jesus, for a house is only as strong as the foundation upon which it stands.

> *Hear my cry, O God, listen to my prayer;*
> *from the end of the earth I call to you*
> *when my heart is faint.*
> *Lead me to the rock that is higher than I . . .*
> **PSALM 61:1–2 (ESV)**

HOMEBUILDING 101:
The Foundation

BALANCE

BUILDING YOUR HOME:

1. In what ways do you struggle to maintain "balance" in your family?

2. How might "balance" look different if you built your home on the rock that is Christ? How would it affect your sense of stability? How might it change the way you manage the stress of being a single mother? Would it transform the way you measure your effectiveness or self-worth?

3. *Life Alignment Activity.* Take a few minutes to create three lists.

List A: Daily/weekly activities. Include work, leisure, rest, housework, time with kids, etc. How much time do you spend on each activity?

List B: Goals. What do you hope to achieve personally over the next five or ten years? Think about areas of education, work, family, finances, character, faith, home, and relationships.

List C: Priorities and Values. What do you value MOST in life?

Once your three lists are complete, check to make sure your activities are in alignment with your goals, priorities, and values. Do you engage in any activities that prevent you from achieving your goals or from becoming who you want to be? Consider removing those activities. Are there any activities that you need to start doing to make sure you are living in accordance with your values and goals? What steps do you need to take to begin?

BUILDING A LEGACY OF FAITH: Study God's Word together
The Bible specifically conveys the importance of sharing God's Word with our children. Consider the following passage:

> *Love the LORD your God with all your heart*
> *and with all your soul and with all your strength.*
> *These commandments that I give you today*
> *are to be on your hearts.*
> *Impress them on your children. Talk about them when*
> *you sit at home and when you walk along the road,*
> *when you lie down and when you get up.*
> *Tie them as symbols on your hands and bind*
> *them on your foreheads.*
> *Write them on the doorframes of your houses*
> *and on your gates.*
> **DEUTERONOMY 6:5–9**

Choose a comforting Scripture from your Bible or from *Building on Solid Ground: "Scriptures for the Single Mother,"* located at the end of this book. Or, you may want to use one of the following Scriptures as a starting point:

Love the LORD your God with all your heart
and with all your soul and with all your strength.
DEUTERONOMY 6:5

"But as for me and my household, we will serve the LORD."
JOSHUA 24:15

Post the Scripture in a highly visible area of your home and discuss its meaning with your children. Locate and underline it in your Bibles. Challenge older children to memorize the verse. School-age children may enjoy a simple journal in which they can write and illustrate their Scriptures and prayers. You may want to choose a new Scripture each month or week. The consistent and purposeful study of God's Word will give you and your children a strong foundation from which to grow.

PART THREE

the
FRAMEWORK

*"The L*ORD *will guide you always;*
he will satisfy your needs in a sun-scorched land
and will strengthen your frame."

ISAIAH 58:11

CHAPTER 4

COMPANIONSHIP

When I feel lonely,
He is my Companion.

*"The LORD himself goes before you and will be with you;
he will never leave you nor forsake you.
Do not be afraid; do not be discouraged."*
DEUTERONOMY 31:8

Three years into my life as a single mother, I worked as a kindergarten teacher and was fortunate enough to have my youngest daughter, Gabrielle, placed in my class as a student. On our morning drive to school, I often asked her random questions to engage in conversation. It was a simple ritual that allowed me to get inside that precocious and precious little-girl mind.

"Mommy, ask me a question," she began one morning near the end of the school year.

"Hmmm. Let me think."

Gabrielle giggled in anticipation. Her wit and wisdom routinely defied her age (five). She was also the smallest in her class. At times, this combination of wit, wisdom, and lack of size was almost too much to bear.

"Gabby, what is the most important thing you think I should know?"

I looked in the rearview mirror to catch her reaction.

"You need to knowwww ..." she began with a grin. *Here it comes. She wants me to buy something. I know that smile.*

"You need to knowwww that God loves you and that He's always with you."

Whew.

How did she know the words my soul longed to hear?

Gabrielle grew silent, as the Holy Spirit descended into the car, piercing my heart with a double-edged sword of truth. *God loves you. He is always with you. YOU ARE NOT ALONE.*

> *"Have I not commanded you?*
> *Be strong and courageous.*
> *Do not be afraid; do not be discouraged,*
> *for the LORD your God will be with you wherever you go."*
> **JOSHUA 1:9**

I struggled to find my breath.

It shouldn't have surprised me. This was the same child who, after crawling into bed with me one night, woke up to see an angel praying over us. "His wings were so white and so long. I worried they might get dirty if they touched the floor," she told me the next morning. "I prayed and prayed and prayed to God, that you would wake up and see the angel too, but you kept sleeping."

As we continued the drive to school, our conversation returned to the normal topics of my five-year-old daughter. But her words stayed with me, turning themselves over and over in my mind. *You need to know that God loves you and that He's always with you.* Although spoken in the voice of a child, those words lifted their mighty weapons and battled the voice of doubt within me—the voice that questioned God's faithfulness.

> *Through the praise of children and infants*
> *you have established a stronghold against your enemies,*
> *to silence the foe and the avenger.*
> **PSALM 8:2**

Gabrielle's message soothed my war-weary soul, allowing me to acknowledge my longing for something more. At the time, I had a relationship with God, albeit a distant one. I prayed, read the Bible occasionally, and taught my girls about God. But I never presumed to have *companionship* with Him. Companionship, I believed, required a level of intimacy, communication, and physical presence better suited for humans. After all, He was GOD—way up *there* somewhere—and I was just little ol' me, all alone, way down *here*. Nothing more than a mere speck in the spectrum of His creation.

> *When I look at your heavens, the work of your fingers,*
> *the moon and the stars, which you have set in place,*
> *what is man that you are mindful of him,*
> *and the son of man that you care for him?*
> **PSALM 8:3-4 (ESV)**

But because God is as patient as He is kind, He continued His holy pursuit of me. Before I could accept His offer of companionship, however, I would first have to wrestle with the doubt of His presence.

THE PERCEPTION OF PRESENCE

It is within our nature as humans to align our perception of God's presence with our current circumstances. In simplest terms, when things work in our favor, we feel God's presence and blessing. When things become difficult, we assume He is distant and perhaps indifferent to our struggles.

As a single mother, I defined myself as profoundly alone. I woke up alone. Went to bed alone. Cared for my children alone. Wrapped Christmas presents alone. Cried alone. This loneliness skewed my perception of God's presence because I unknowingly blamed Him for my feelings of isolation and abandonment. And my unanswered prayers for the companionship of a husband only intensified my perception of God's distance and indifference. I now understand that God, in His infinite mercy, allowed me to wait for a husband so that *He might become my Unseen Companion*—my first love. But it would take God eight long years to convince me of His presence. I was not easily swayed.

> *The LORD is near to all who call on him,*
> *to all who call on him in truth.*
> **PSALM 145:18**

Instead of calling *on* God and asking for His presence, I typically called Him *out*, accusing Him of distance. Perhaps this is why, out of all the writers of the Bible, I identified most closely with David of the Psalms. When dealing with danger, betrayal, pain, and the consequences of our sin, we both felt compelled to pick up our pen and question God's presence.

*Why, L*ORD*, do you stand far off? Why do you hide yourself in times of trouble?*

DAVID, PSALM 10:1

*How long, L*ORD*? Will you forget me forever? How long will you hide your face from me?*

DAVID, PSALM 13:1

My God, my God, why have you forsaken me? Why are you so far from saving me, so far from my cries of anguish?

DAVID, PSALM 22:1

Lord, where ARE you in this?

ME, IN NUMEROUS JOURNAL ENTRIES AND PRAYERS

Like most people, David and I did not base our accusations on truth but rather on our ever-changing perception of God's presence, fueled by intense emotion and limited understanding. Thankfully, David, far wiser than I, set a powerful example, which transformed the way I communicated with God. While writing his Psalms of lament, David usually followed a pattern: a direct address to God, a complaint, a plea for help, a statement of trust, and finally, an expression of overflowing praise.

David's ability to pour out his unabashed grievances before God modeled a level of comfort typically reserved for the closest of relationships. I learned that I didn't have to pull myself together before going to God. He could handle my authentic and unedited emotion. David's ability to then curb his feelings by returning to trust and praise demonstrated a deep respect for God as Sovereign King. This taught me that acknowledging God's character, authority, and strength brought me to a place of peace and security. David's companionship with God encompassed both the comfort found in familiarity and the humility found in respect.

David, who felt secure enough to question God's nearness, penned some of the most eloquent and impactful Scriptures in all of the Bible—words that convey a Holy Presence, far beyond our human reasoning.

> *Where can I go from your Spirit?*
> *Where can I flee from your presence?*
> *If I go up to the heavens, you are there;*
> *if I make my bed in the depths, you are there.*
> *If I rise on the wings of the dawn,*
> *if I settle on the far side of the sea,*
> *even there your hand will guide me,*
> *your right hand will hold me fast.*
> **PSALM 139:7-10**

As we grow in our companionship with God, it is imperative to understand that our limited perception of His presence rarely aligns with the fullness of His Truth. God remains GOD, no matter our circumstances. He is the Creator of heaven and earth. The Beginning and the End. Father to the fatherless. Holy. Mighty. Sovereign. Perfect and Transcendent in all of His ways. He is Omnipresent (in all places, at all times), Omniscient (in full knowledge of everything), and Omnipotent (all-powerful). And though *Unseen*, He remains eternally *Present*.

"Who can hide in secret places so that I cannot see them?"
declares the LORD.
"Do not I fill heaven and earth?"
JEREMIAH 23:24

THE CHOICE OF COMPANIONSHIP

Now that we've dealt with our perception of His presence, we come to one of the most gracious and somewhat confounding gifts from God—the choice of companionship. God does not force Himself on anyone. While He stands ever near, hidden only behind a thin veil, God allows us to determine our closeness with Him.

As our Creator, God holds complete knowledge of us. He knows every word on our tongue and the number of hairs on our head. He knows each sin, victory, dream, and wound. God is acquainted with all of our ways, both seen and unseen. *Yet* we determine the depth of intimacy in our relationship with Him—how much we are willing to share and how well we get to know Him.

He recorded each day of our existence in His Book of Life before one of them came to be. *But* we exert free will in how we spend each of those days and if we will spend any of them with Him.

God continually works on our behalf and for our good, storing up unimaginable treasures in heaven for us. *However*, we control the extent of His influence over our earthly lives.

God remains eternally steadfast in love, nearness, availability, and want of us. So strong are His affections and desire for us that He sent His only Son as an atoning sacrifice for our sins. *And we retain the right to accept or reject Jesus as our Savior.*

Our Father and King stands before us with arms open wide, inviting us into companionship with Him. With that companionship, we gain not only our salvation, but also the gifts, privileges, and treasures available to us as Daughters and Heirs to the Kingdom. We only have one requirement to receive; we must draw near to Him to accept His gift.

Draw near to God, and he will draw near to you.
JAMES 4:8 (ESV)

Some of us will run to our Companion with unwavering faith and expectation.

Others will draw only near enough to receive salvation, but with eyes clouded by distractions of the world, they will miss the gift of close companionship.

And some will reject Him altogether.

She does not trust in the LORD, she does not
draw near to her God.
ZEPHANIAH 3:2

But God remains GOD— eternally *Present* and close beside us. He remains faithful, merciful, and kind, as He patiently awaits the day we call out His name.

THE GIFT OF COMPANIONSHIP

Let us draw near to God with a sincere heart and with the
full assurance that faith brings . . .
HEBREWS 10:22

After nearly nine years of being a single mother, I met a man who shared my love for God, ministry, and education. A couple of years after we married, we directed a Christian camp for at-risk, inner-city children. After a few days of hiking, singing, and learning about God's Word, we felt a stirring among the kids. They longed for a deeper authenticity. They began telling their stories and asking tougher questions about faith. They desperately wanted God but didn't understand where He was in the midst of their adult-sized issues.

To demonstrate what a relationship with God might look like, we asked a teen counselor to stand in front of the room as a representation of God. He held a wrapped present in his hands, symbolizing God's gift of salvation, love, and companionship.

"Boys and girls, we are going to create a tableau, or a frozen picture, of a relationship with God. Some of us might feel very close Him." I moved myself close to the young man posing as God. "We might even be ready to accept His gift of love. Some of us might feel far away from God."

I then asked the kids to think about where they were in proximity to God and called for volunteers to "act it out."

One by one, kids came forward and placed themselves accordingly. I still tear up, remembering their remarkable courage and honesty as they created this frozen picture of relationship. One child knelt down near God and raised his hands toward the gift. Another stood a little further away with her arms crossed and back toward God. One stood to the side and pretended to engage in conversation with God, and yet another child moved himself to the far end of the room, seemingly out of sight.

Children who did not volunteer whispered to their friends where they would stand. It was beginning to sink in. We all have different responses to His gift of companionship. Just when I was ready to end the lesson and send students back to their places, my daughter Gabrielle raised her hand. "Can I go?" she asked. I had no idea where she would place herself. My daughter, now twelve years old, whose heart burned in longing for her absent father. My daughter, who struggled with loyalty issues as she grew to love her stepfather. *Where would she place herself in proximity to God, the Father?*

Gabrielle made her way to the front of the room, took the gift out of God's hands and set it down. Then, without any warning, she leaped into His arms. And as God held my Gabrielle, with His arms wrapped tightly around her, she rested her head on His chest and closed her eyes.

> *Let the beloved of the LORD rest secure in him,*
> *for he shields him all day long,*
> *and the one the LORD loves rests between his shoulders.*
> **DEUTERONOMY 33:12**

There were a few audible gasps in the room; then everyone grew silent for a moment as they contemplated what had just happened. One girl, unable to contain herself any longer, blurted out, "That's what I want!"

Isn't that what we all want? A companionship so intimate, we can run to God in confident expectation, leap into His arms, and trust in His willingness to hold us.

> *"And surely I am with you always, to the very end of the age."*
> **MATTHEW 28:20**

HOMEBUILDING 101:
The Framework

COMPANIONSHIP

BUILDING YOUR HOME:

1. What is your *perception* of God's *presence* in your life?

2. Read Psalm 139. What does this Scripture tell us about the *truth* of God's *presence*?

3. What is your *proximity* to God? Imagine, for a moment, where you stand in relationship to God at this time of your life. How close are you? What is your posture? And more importantly, where would you like to be in companionship with God?

DRAWING CLOSER TO GOD:

God created us to be relational people. While Jesus was on earth, He lived in companionship with others. They traveled and ate together. As Jesus taught, His followers asked questions and engaged in meaningful conversations with Him and amongst each other. They *knew* Him.

> *Draw near to God, and he will draw near to you.*
> **JAMES 4:8 (ESV)**

Even the occasional prayer and acknowledgment of God's presence is powerful enough to reduce fear and loneliness in times of distress. Spending purposeful time with God in prayer and His Word, however, can elevate our relationship with Him to be the most important in our life.

Other ways to draw close to God may include:

- Keeping a prayer journal
- Talking to God throughout the day about all areas of your life
- Underlining important Scriptures in your Bible
- Placing key Scriptures throughout your house as reminders of God's love and presence

Think about the differences between the various tableaus the students created at camp. When Gabrielle drew near to God and jumped into His arms without hesitation, the level of intimacy changed dramatically. She chose to trust in His ability to catch her and His willingness to hold her close.

4. What is your level of trust with God?

5. In what areas of life do you need to jump into His arms and allow Him to hold you?

BUILDING A LEGACY OF FAITH: Join a community of believers

And let us consider how we may spur one another on
toward love and good deeds,
not giving up meeting together, as some are in
the habit of doing,
but encouraging one another—
HEBREWS 10:24-25

After my divorce, I stopped going to church regularly, justifying it with the excuse that I was too tired and busy. While that was true, I was more worried about being judged by those who seemed to have the "perfect Christian life," devoid of complicated issues such as mine. But, after my conversation with Gabrielle when she told me, "You need to know that God loves you and that He is always with you," I realized that both my children and I needed to develop a stronger relationship with God and His people. I reached out to the women's pastor at my local church, who listened as I poured out my story in all its shame and wretched truth. She listened to my worry, regret, longing, and doubt. She wrapped her arms around me and spoke of God's love, presence, and forgiveness.

And at that moment, she became the church as God intended. I no longer worried about the opinions of others because I knew I stood within the grace and forgiveness of Jesus. Returning to a church family gave my daughters and me the love, support, accountability, and encouragement we desperately needed.

CHAPTER 5

PROVISION

When I am in need,
He is my Provider.

I detested checking the mailbox every day. Other than the occasional card from my grandmother, my mailbox contained two types of mail. Junk and bills. One served as a reminder of what I couldn't afford, and the other of what I had yet to pay. And both offered my daily dose of shame. I usually threw the junk mail into the trash and placed the unopened envelopes in a box beside my desk. The bills would have to wait.

But one day, an unexpected letter came from my church—the first church to show me God's love for single mothers.

After several years of absence, I found myself pulled back within the folds of the church, thanks to the listening ear and welcoming arms of the women's pastor. At her urging, I joined the single mothers' ministry, which offered spiritual support, friendship, and tangible help. Once I became a mentor, she asked me to share my story with the other single mothers, focusing on the new identity I found in Christ. I assumed the envelope contained a simple thank-you note.

Dear Michelle:

Enclosed is a check that will hopefully encourage you on your journey. Recently some funds were given to the church for the benefit of several single moms and, as requested, we are forwarding a portion of those funds to you. I pray you experience the love that precipitated this gift, and that you will prayerfully determine the best use of these dollars. May God continue to bless you and your family.

In Him,

LifeBridge Christian Church

The envelope contained a check for $1,000.

And my God will meet all your needs
according to the riches of his glory in Christ Jesus.
PHILIPPIANS 4:19

I fell onto the floor in a wailing heap of gratitude, clutching the letter to my chest. I had never before experienced the lavish and unexpected abundance of God.

It took a moment to collect myself enough to convince my daughters, who had joined me on the floor, that Mommy was just crying "happy tears." All was well.

All was truly well.

That evening, I worked for hours on the budget, prayerfully rationing money for our immediate needs—winter coats for the girls, a seriously overdue utility bill, and extra canned goods and frozen food for the winter. Although there were plenty of bills yet to pay, I set aside $200 to start an emergency fund. My mind reeled at the wonder and timing of this gift because I hadn't shared the details of financial distress with anyone at church.

No one knew that in my desperation to buy food for my children, I had recently returned a jacket to Walmart with a $24 price tag still attached. No one knew I bit my lip almost to the point of drawing blood, as the girls and I then shopped for two weeks worth of groceries with a measly $12 because the jacket had gone on sale since my purchase.

No one knew the times my daughters and I ate a cold dinner by candlelight because our electricity was shut off for non-payment, or that the county had rejected my application for childcare assistance and food stamps because I made $300 over the income limit.

No one knew my auto insurance had lapsed the same month as my car accident, or how its subsequent consequences catapulted me into bankruptcy and financial ruin.

No one knew the apprehension that prevented me from legally pursuing the child support my children deserved.

And no one knew I had finally broken down in prayer just a week earlier, pleading with God for help and confessing my financial failures, fears, and inadequacies. No one saw the fistful of change I put in the offering basket that Sunday to show God I trusted Him with all I had.

No one knew. *But God did.*

The Issue with Need

I am nothing but skin and bones . . .
JOB 19:20

Let's be real here. No one has ever accused me of being "skin and bones," as my dress size would attest. While I struggled as a single mother to provide for my family's basic needs, we never knew a day of *real* hunger. We had regular access to shelter, food, water, clothing, transportation, employment, education, technology, utilities, and medical care. If we lacked any basic need, it was usually temporary.

By the numbers, my single-parent family fit within the classification of "lower-middle class." The threat of falling into "situational poverty," however, loomed every day. Situational poverty occurs when an unexpected crisis or demand depletes one's limited financial resources, causing them to fall temporarily below the poverty line and lose access to basic necessities. Factors contributing to the situational poverty of a single mother might include underemployment or loss of employment, lack of child support, lawyer fees, illness or medical emergency, vehicle repairs, Christmas and birthdays, back-to-school supplies and clothes, and the payments or fees associated with mismanaged finances.

I experienced *frequent* falls into situational poverty. It was not uncommon for my bank account to be nearly emptied by the third week of each month, leaving almost nothing for food and gas for the following weeks. When payday finally arrived, I immediately spent money on food, rent, utilities, and gas to regain a sense of security. This vicious cycle repeated month after month, year after year, leaving me in a constant state of need, vulnerability, instability, and desperation—leaving me as "skin and bones."

I know many of you, if not most, can relate. And some of you are experiencing, at this moment, a level of poverty and deprivation I will never fully understand. Know that I pray for all of you as I write on this sensitive topic and desperately wish I had the words or financial "formula" to ease your burden. The issues pertaining to single mothers and money are complicated and far-reaching, certainly deserving of an entire book. For the purposes of this chapter, however, we will focus on the spiritual aspects of poverty and provision.

THE SPIRIT OF POVERTY

"You earn wages, only to put them in a purse with holes in it."
HAGGAI 1:6

As a single mother, I struggled in my longing for self-sufficiency and the reality of my insufficiency. Having been told (and convinced) I was a "weight" and "burden" in my old life, I entered my new life as a single mother determined to prove my worth through a grand display of independence. I dreamed of purchasing a little home and creating a beautiful refuge for my family. I planned to provide my children with opportunities and vacations denied in our old life. But after years of unmet needs, lack of child support, and frequent falls into situational poverty, I stopped dreaming. No longer striving to prove my self-sufficiency, I simply fought to survive.

And at some point, after I had grown weary enough, I defined myself as *poor*, and the world as a place of *scarcity*. I took this belief into my spirit, allowing its tendrils to wrap themselves around each area of my life, and soon everything seemed of short supply. Money. Love. Ability. Grace. Beauty. Knowledge. Time. Sleep. Joy. Friends. Faith. Blessings.

Some define this perception as a "poverty mindset" or a "scarcity mentality," a negative pattern of thinking and speaking that perpetuates a continual state of lack. Because this mentality has a pervasive influence over our faith, I refer to it as a "Spirit of Poverty." By "spirit," I do not imply it involves an evil spirit or demon that needs to be cast out. Rather, "spirit" refers to the inner being of a person—the hidden chambers that house one's character, emotions, beliefs, and perceptions. Allowing the poverty or scarcity mindset to seep into our spirit taints not only our perception of the world, but also of God, and serves as a form of bondage that prevents us from embracing a life of abundance.

"I came that they may have life and have it abundantly."
—JOHN 10:10 (ESV)

The Spirit of Poverty is not a new phenomenon. In the Book of Haggai in the Old Testament, God confronts His people about their priorities. In 538 BC, fifty thousand exiled Jews were allowed to return to Jerusalem to rebuild the temple. Also known as the house of God or God's dwelling place, the temple served as a holy place of communion between God and His people. While the people understood the importance of rebuilding the temple, they did not understand its future significance. Upon its completion, this temple would not only house the Spirit of God, but it would someday house the physical manifestation of God—when, hundreds of years later, Mary and Joseph would bring baby Jesus, the long-awaited Messiah, to this temple for His dedication.

The people rebuilt the temple foundation within two years and rejoiced upon its completion. But feeling pressure from neighboring regions, they stopped their work. They focused their efforts, instead, on building their own houses, leaving the house of God unfinished.

Through the prophet Haggai, God asked:

"Is it a time for you yourselves to be living in
your paneled houses,
while this house remains a ruin? . . .
Give careful thought to your ways.
You have planted much, but harvested little.
You eat, but never have enough.
You drink, but never have your fill.
You put on clothes, but are not warm.
You earn wages, only to put them
in a purse with holes in it."

HAGGAI 1:4–6

Though His people worked hard and lived in lavish homes, they failed to prosper. Abandoning the house of God left them in a constant state of depravity and want.

"You expected much, but see, it turned out to be little.
What you brought home, I blew away. Why?"
declares the LORD Almighty.
"Because of my house, which remains a ruin,
while each of you is busy with your own house."

HAGGAI 1:9

But how does this Scripture relate to the single mother? Does it imply that God "blows away" her provisions as a punishment? Certainly not. This Scripture does not speak of punishment but rather the longing God has to dwell with His people. So great is His longing, God sent the Holy Spirit to live *within* us after the death and resurrection of Jesus.

Don't you know that you yourselves are God's temple
and that God's Spirit dwells in your midst?

1 CORINTHIANS 3:16

We are now the temple—the house of God. If we neglect to build the temple beyond its foundation and focus instead on the things of this world, we choose a spiritually impoverished life. In other words, if our faith stops at the point of our salvation and we fail to grow in companionship and knowledge of God, we miss out on His overflowing abundance. Like a thirsty woman drawing from the well, we forget the Living Water available to us.

"Be strong, all you people of the land," declares the LORD, "and work. For I am with you," declares the LORD Almighty. ". . . And my Spirit remains among you. Do not fear."
HAGGAI 2:4-5

After God had confronted His people for neglecting the temple, He reminded them of His presence and encouraged them to build again. God promised His blessing in return and assured them He would fill the new temple with His glory and peace.

And so it is with us. When we shift our focus away from the want of this world, and build the temple within us, we receive His blessing and peace. We exchange our Spirit of Poverty for a Spirit of Abundance. Instead of concentrating on our small apartment, old clothing, and lack of a savings account, we are more inclined to thank God for housing our soul, clothing us in righteousness, and storing treasures for us in heaven. This change of perspective dramatically changes the way we receive the blessings of this life, both large and small.

Overcoming the Spirit of Poverty

Do not conform to the pattern of this world, but be transformed by the renewing of your mind.
ROMANS 12:2

To overcome the Spirit of Poverty, we must first recognize the powerful influence this mindset has over our belief in God as a Provider. Because this belief system causes us to view life through the lens of scarcity, we unknowingly project limitations on God's ability and willingness to provide for us. Embracing the Word of God as *Truth* allows us to break this stronghold. Below are several misperceptions and truths about God's role as our Provider.

Misperception: God has limited knowledge. He doesn't know what I need.

Truth: *"Your Father knows what you need before you ask him"* (Matt. 6:8).

Misperception: God has limited ability. He doesn't have the power to give me everything I need. It's out of His control.

Truth: *Now to him who is able to do immeasurably more than all we ask or imagine, according to his power that is at work within us, to him be glory in the church and in Christ Jesus throughout all generations, for ever and ever! Amen* (Eph. 3:20–21).

Misperception: God has limited love. He is deliberately withholding His blessing from me. He doesn't love me.

Truth: *"Ask and it will be given to you; seek and you will find; knock and the door will be opened to you. For everyone who asks receives; the one who seeks finds; and to the one who knocks, the* *door will be opened. Which of you, if your son asks for bread, will give him a stone? Or if he asks for a fish, will give him a snake? If you, then, though you are evil, know how to give good gifts to your children, how much more will your Father in heaven give good gifts to those who ask him!"* (Matt. 7:7–11)

He who did not spare his own Son, but gave him up for us all—how will he not also, along with him, graciously give us all things? (Rom. 8:32)

Misperception: God has limited grace. He knows I don't deserve help. He expects me to be responsible and fix my own problems.

Truth: *And hope does not put us to shame, because God's love has been poured out into our hearts through the Holy Spirit, who has been given to us. You see, at just the right time, when we were still powerless, Christ died for the ungodly* (Rom. 5:5–6).

THE POVERTY OF JESUS

Even as we begin to recognize God as our Provider, it is natural to assume He does not fully understand what we are going through. After all, how could God, who holds the riches of both heaven and earth, possibly comprehend need? He might see our poverty from afar, as one views the moon through a telescope, but does He know how it *feels*?

Often known as the Great Exchange, Jesus' death on the cross served as an atoning sacrifice for our sins, giving us salvation and a new life in Him. He took on our sin in exchange for His righteousness. But did you know, there was another "Great Exchange" at the cross? Jesus took on our *poverty* in exchange for His *riches*.

For you know the grace of our Lord Jesus Christ,
that though he was rich, yet for your sake he became poor,
so that you through his poverty might become rich.
2 CORINTHIANS 8:9

When Jesus died on the cross, He was:

Hungry: *"I have eagerly desired to eat this Passover with you before I suffer. For I tell you, I will not eat it again until it finds fulfillment in the kingdom of God"* (Luke 22:15–16).

Thirsty: *"I am thirsty"* (John 19:28).

Naked: *When the soldiers crucified Jesus, they took his clothes, dividing them into four shares, one for each of them* (John 19:23).

Abandoned: *About three in the afternoon Jesus cried out in a loud voice, "Eli, Eli, lema sabachthani?" (which means "My God, my God, why have you forsaken me?")* (Matt. 27:46).

And being laid to rest in a borrowed tomb, He was homeless. *"Foxes have dens and birds have nests, but the Son of Man has no place to lay his head"* (Matt. 8:20).

Jesus chose to carry our poverty into the grave, that we might receive His glorious riches. If we believe the Word of God is true, we have no reason to carry the Spirit of Poverty within us any longer. Jesus paid our debt and said, *"It is finished"* (John 19:30).

EMBRACING THE SPIRIT OF ABUNDANCE

I have learned to be content whatever the circumstances.
I know what it is to be in need, and I know
what it is to have plenty.
I have learned the secret of being content
in any and every situation,

whether well fed or hungry, whether living
in plenty or in want.
I can do all this through him who gives me strength.
PHILIPPIANS 4:11-13

Oh, friends, the lavishness of God still overwhelms me. When I finally laid down my Spirit of Poverty at the foot of the cross and received a Spirit of Abundance in exchange, it was as though a curtain had been lifted from my eyes. Instead of pleading, "God, where ARE you in this?" I found myself marveling, "Oh God, I SEE YOU in this!" His abundance was evident.

"One thing I do know. I was blind but now I see!"
JOHN 9:25

This new perspective had nothing to do with financial stability. God did not pay off my debt or buy a house or give me a winning lotto ticket. He did not always answer my prayers in the way I hoped, and quite honestly, I still struggled to provide for my family. But instead of focusing on the sparse supply of food in the refrigerator, my daughters and I thanked God for the abundance on our plate. Instead of feeling panic when I checked my bank account balance, I found security knowing my Provider was near.

Although I didn't realize it until much later, my daughters received the greatest gift found in God's abundance—a new legacy. For their mother no longer engaged the world with the empty hands of a beggar, but as one whose hands overflowed with God's abundance. And children know what's in their momma's hands.

HOMEBUILDING 101:
The Framework

PROVISION

BUILDING YOUR HOME:

1. Do you feel comfortable acknowledging your needs, weaknesses, insecurities, and fears before God? If not, why is this difficult for you?

2. What perceptions do you have about God's ability and willingness to provide for you and your children?

3. How has God provided for you in the past?

4. What do you need to request of Him now?

ASKING GOD FOR PROVISION:

One way to make requests of God is to follow the example of Jesus in the Lord's Prayer, found in Matthew 6:9–13.

1. Acknowledge God and His sovereignty. (See also 2 Corinthians 9:8.)

Our Father in heaven, hallowed be your name.

2. Submit to God's will for your life. (See also Luke 22:42.)
Your kingdom come, your will be done, on earth as it is in heaven.

3. Make your request of God. (See also John 16:23–24, Matt. 7:7, and Phil. 4:6.)
Give us today our daily bread.

4. Ask for forgiveness so nothing may hinder your prayers. (See also Mark 11:22–25.)
And forgive us our debts, as we also have forgiven our debtors.

5. Ask for protection for you and your family.
And lead us not into temptation, but deliver us from the evil one.

BUILDING A LEGACY OF FAITH: Count your blessings

In my early years of being a single mother, I often made the mistake of telling my children we were "poor" and couldn't afford their requested item. Although I didn't realize it at the time, my choice of words birthed the spirit of poverty within them. Once I realized this harmful impact, I immediately changed the way I spoke about money in front of my children. If we were in the store and the girls wanted to purchase something I couldn't afford, I no longer spoke about being poor or broke. Instead, I'd convey the importance of making wise choices with the money we *did* have by saying, "That doesn't fall within the budget today" or "That isn't on the list." Sometimes, I would engage my daughter's help in making choices between certain items or challenging them to find the better deal.

Many children of single mothers identify themselves as poor and needy. As parents, we can reverse this spirit of poverty in our children by cultivating an environment of thanksgiving and gratitude in our home. While there are countless ways to express thanks, begin by modeling a heart of gratitude. Thank your children for the small things. Allow them to hear you express your gratefulness to God for the blessings in your life. Start a gratitude jar or journal for your children to document their blessings. I smile as I remember an activity that my daughters both loved and despised. When the bickering started during long car trips, we played the "Thankfulness Game," in which we each took turns saying the things for which we were thankful. After about fifty expressions of gratitude, their attitudes changed.

CHAPTER 6

HEALING

When I am in pain,
He is my Healer.

He heals the brokenhearted and binds up their wounds.
PSALM 147:3

Near the upper reaches of the subalpine tree line in the Rocky Mountains, the freezing wind blows with such violence that trees grow parallel to the earth. Known for their twisted and gnarled appearance, wind-sculpted Krummholtz trees (German for "crooked or bent wood") actually move across the tundra in a will to survive. As exposed, wind-beaten tissue dies off, new growth and roots establish themselves on the protected side of the tree, slowly pulling it forward in a vain attempt to escape its aggressor. These horizontal pillars of strength can survive several hundred to over a thousand years simply by keeping their head down.

I feel a great kinship to those bent-back trees. We both endured a wind that buffeted and bent our lives, but we continued to grow and move forward, digging our roots into the frozen earth below.

My "wind" began like most—a constant breeze with a few

occasional gusts. Life presented me with its typical struggles and challenges, and I took pride in my ability to withstand the flurries. I called it flexibility. I knew that being a Christian would not exempt me from the harsh realities of this world, so I leaned into the promises found in God's Word and committed myself to learn the lessons each "flurry" offered.

Not only so, but we also glory in our sufferings,
because we know that suffering produces perseverance;
perseverance, character;
and character, hope.
ROMANS 5:3-4

Then the real storm started. Like the Krummholtz trees that grew prostrate on the ground, the "wind" in my life grew to such strength, I could no longer recover while emotionally upright. I found no rest, no reprieve, no shelter from the tempest. I doubted God's promise that suffering would produce perseverance, character, and hope. With a bent back and eyes facing the ground, I walked through the minutes of each day, hoping merely to survive each storm.

On a Sabbath Jesus was teaching in one of the synagogues,
and a woman was there who had been crippled
by a spirit for eighteen years.
She was bent over and could not straighten up at all.
When Jesus saw her, he called her forward and said to her,
"Woman, you are set free from your infirmity."
Then he put his hands on her,
and immediately she straightened up and praised God.
LUKE 13:10-13

A *spirit* crippled the woman. Derived from the Greek word *pneuma*, "spirit" means breath, spirit, or *wind*. Like the tree, a constant and debilitating "wind" bent the back of this woman, binding her for eighteen years. The Greek language in this text indicates that her illness not only caused physical suffering, but it also rendered her dependent and helpless, depriving her of the ability to contribute. Unable to lift her eyes to heaven, she held little hope for healing. She felt constant pain, and the dusty ground beneath her feet offered the only beauty she saw in life. Though the community likely overlooked and ostracized this woman, Jesus saw her. He saw the bondage of both her body and spirit and called her forward. Through the power of His word and touch, He released the crippled woman from the "wind" that tormented her, allowing her to look once again to heaven and rejoice.

Jesus continues to heal bent-back women today.

TIES THAT BIND

The cords of death entangled me,
the anguish of the grave came over me;
I was overcome by distress and sorrow.
PSALM 116:3

One Saturday morning when I was nine or ten years old, my father extended a rare invitation to go fishing. Delighted to spend time with him, I rested my fishing pole on my shoulder and whistled as we walked to the stream, mimicking Opie in the opening scene of "The Andy Griffith Show." While my father remained on the trail, I meandered around the pine trees, dipped under branches, jumped over rocks, and explored every inch of the forest within ten feet of the path. Without warning, something yanked me backward with enough force to make me fall.

Apparently, my hook and line had gotten caught somewhere on the trail behind us, and as we walked, my reel had silently emptied itself of an entire spool of line. I think I learned every swear word that day as my father and I collected over 150 yards of fishing line, retracing my steps around pine trees, under branches, over rocks . . . and across every inch of the forest within ten feet of the trail. For some reason, I have no memory of actually fishing that day.

Unhealed emotional wounds and unconfessed sin work much in the same way as they bind us with an invisible line to those people or circumstances that hurt us.

A "tie that binds" is a strong emotional connection to a person, place, experience, or sin that, when triggered, affects our feelings, behavior, and belief systems. Such ties can be either positive or negative. For example, when I hear the sound of an acoustic guitar, I immediately feel a sensation of warmth and security. Whether or not I realize it at the time, the guitar triggers an emotional response, revealing a near-invisible tie that binds me to my mother and the hours I spent sitting at her knee while she sang and played the guitar.

In contrast, the smell of Scotch whisky makes me lose my breath. My heart races if I realize I forgot to lock the door in the middle of the night. And although I no longer stand in the direct path of the torrential "wind," a harsh word immediately bends my back.

Shake off your dust; rise up, sit enthroned, Jerusalem.
Free yourself from the chains on your neck,
Daughter Zion, now a captive.
ISAIAH 52:2

Just as God calls us to release our spirit of poverty to receive His abundance, He also calls us to remove the ties that bind us to old wounds so that we might receive His healing. The Bible refers to these ties as *chains around our neck, cords of death, cords of affliction,* and *burdensome yoke*s, each expression symbolizing an emotional or spiritual bondage, or slavery, to sin.

The first step in removing these harmful ties is to recognize their source. This presents a problem because "ties that bind" often remain largely unnoticed. We believe we react to life's circumstances with particular quirks and responses, unique to our personality, when in actuality, our responses may be related to wounding. We might overreact to being startled accidentally. Or perhaps we have a habit of falling in love with the wrong kind of men. Maybe a certain smell or sound triggers a moment of panic. Being able to link our uncomfortable or inappropriate responses to a source helps us to release the ties that keep us in emotional bondage.

It is for freedom that Christ has set us free.
Stand firm, then, and do not let yourselves be burdened
again by a yoke of slavery.
GALATIANS 5:1

For every "tie that binds," there is an origin, a trigger, and a response. Just as my father and I retraced 150 yards of fishing line until we found the tree that caught the hook, we must retrace our steps to determine the origin of our emotional responses.

1. Identify the unwanted response. When do you feel overwhelming and uncontrollable emotion? What do you avoid? Where do you feel most out of control in your life? While there are hundreds of possibilities, consider the following list below, and determine an area in which you struggle.

My example of a response: fear-based decisions and avoidance. Although I love singing and have considerable experience, I feel petrified if I think anyone might hear me. I sing quietly in church and haven't sung on stage for years.

Origin	Trigger	Response
		overwhelming emotion
		fear-based decisions
		avoidance
		agression/anger
		anxiety
		poor choices
		learned helplessness
		recklessness
		detachment
		substance abuse

2. Identify the trigger. A trigger is an experience that consciously or unconsciously reminds us of a prior event. A trigger evokes an involuntary emotional response, whether or not it is directly related to the original circumstance. Think about the unwanted response you identified. Where were you? What were you doing?

My example of a trigger: place and event. I feel nervous and self-conscious while singing during worship at church and when someone extends the opportunity to sing in public places.

Origin	Trigger	Response
	place	overwhelming emotion
	time	fear-based decisions
	event	avoidance
	senses	agression/anger
	conversation	anxiety
	interaction with others	poor choices
	familiar situation	learned helplessness
	anniversary of event	recklessness
	temptation	detachment
		substance abuse

3. Identify the origin. Once we identify the trigger, we move backwards in time, exploring the possible origins of our emotional bondage.

My example of an "origin": I remember a painful experience in which I sang in a music competition in front of Christian recording executives. I sang well but went fifteen seconds over my time limit. In the crowded room, the judge informed me of my disqualification, "We liked it, just not that much of it." I packed my voice and his words like baggage and left the room. From that day on, I sang in whispers.

Origin	Trigger	Response
loss	place	overwhelming emotion
childhood memory	time	fear-based decisions
physical injury	event	avoidance
emotional trauma	senses	agression/anger
physical abuse	conversation	anxiety
sexual abuse	interaction with others	poor choices
verbal abuse	familiar situation	learned helplessness
neglect	anniversary of event	recklessness
poverty	temptation	detachment
bullying		substance abuse
difficult conversations		
abusive words		
sin		

4. Break the "tie that binds" with truth, prayer, and forgiveness. Once the origin is determined, we break our bondage by telling ourselves the truth, praying, and offering (or seeking) forgiveness.

My example of breaking a "tie that binds":

Tell myself the truth: I received criticism in a singing competition years ago. It has no bearing on the quality of my voice today or the perception others will feel about my singing. I merely went over my time limit.

Prayer and forgiveness: Though the judge's words engraved themselves into my heart, I release them to You, God. It seems silly to forgive him. It happened long ago, and he probably didn't intend to hurt me. But I choose to forgive him in an effort to break free from this bondage of shame. Please help me to overcome my fear of being heard so that I might once again find joy in speaking and singing. Help me to find my voice. Amen.

5. Receive God's healing. Soon after I prayed, God restored my courage to sing in front of an audience, and I eventually performed lead roles in several musicals. While I still feel the temptation to shy away from singing today, I no longer remain crippled in fear. I identify the trigger when it hits, remember the origin, and respond according to present day circumstances, rather than those of long ago.

> *They did not realize it was I who healed them.*
> *I led them with cords of human kindness, with ties of love.*
> **HOSEA 11:3–4**

From origin to response: While the example I chose is relatively minor compared to the deep emotional ties I've severed, it serves as a good example of how to follow an unwanted response back to its origin. But sometimes, we must begin with the *origin* and move forward. We may know *exactly* where the source of our pain lies, remembering each wretched detail. We remember how old we were, what we were wearing, who hurt us, and what happened. We remember each word spoken, tear, and silent prayer for healing, but eventually, we set it aside as nothing more than a bookmark in our life. While we recognize it as a source of pain, we fail to recognize its influence over our behaviors, beliefs, and habits today. In this case, we must begin with the origin, and move forward to recognize and break free from our bondage.

Seeking help: Many "ties that bind" are relatively easy to break once identified. It simply becomes a matter of telling ourselves the truth, petitioning God in prayer, offering forgiveness, and receiving God's healing. Some wounding, however, keeps us so enslaved in mind, body, and spirit that we must seek professional help to break free and find healing.

The bent-back woman, mentioned earlier in the chapter, did not possess the strength or ability to heal herself. She required the help of a professional Healer.

> *When Jesus saw her, he called her forward and said to her,*
> *"Woman, you are set free from your infirmity."*
> **LUKE 13:12**

We know an evil spirit bent the back of the woman, keeping her crippled for eighteen years until Jesus set her free. The word for "set free" in the original Greek text is *luó*, meaning to "untie, loosen, release, break, destroy, or unbind." In other words, Jesus not only healed her physical body, but He also released her from the bondage that crippled her spirit. Immediately upon being healed, the woman stood straight and praised God.

Unhealed wounding not only causes emotional and physical pain; it also prevents us from receiving the abundant life that is in Jesus. Professional help is sometimes a necessary step in finding our healing and abundance. Seeking help is not a sign of weakness, nor should it be a source of shame or embarrassment. According to God's Word, obtaining counsel is a sign of wisdom and strength.

> *Let the wise listen and add to their learning,*
> *and let the discerning get guidance—*
> **PROVERBS 1:5**

Please seek immediate help from a professional if you or your children:

- Suffer from prolonged depression, anxiety, or feelings of helplessness
- Engage in risky, dangerous, or out-of-control behaviors
- Abuse alcohol, drugs, sex, or food
- Currently experience or have a history of emotional, physical, spiritual, or sexual abuse
- Engage in self-harm
- Have suicidal thoughts
- Feel unable to physically or verbally control anger towards others

FORGIVENESS

> *Bear with each other and forgive one another*
> *if any of you has a grievance against someone.*
> *Forgive as the Lord forgave you.*
> **COLOSSIANS 3:13**

Offering forgiveness: I knew God called me to forgive, but I held righteous anger in my hands as one holds their money. *This is mine. I earned it. I am entitled to spend it as I deem fit!* I argued with God, reminding Him I had a *right* to feel angry. Embittered. Resentful and furious. After all, my daughters and I were the *victims.*

Victimization and learned helplessness are pervasive and destructive forms of bondage for single mothers. When we withhold forgiveness and continue to blame someone or something else for our "lot in life," we forfeit our right to freedom. We remain tied to the offender, giving them control over our emotions and choices. When we forgive, on the other hand, we forfeit our "right" to continue blaming that person for our circumstances. God calls us to forgive, whether or not the offender seeks or deserves our forgiveness, because it releases our bondage and empowers us to take responsibility for our lives.

Get rid of all bitterness, rage and anger,
brawling and slander, along with every form of malice.
Be kind and compassionate to one another,
forgiving each other, just as in Christ God forgave you.
EPHESIANS 4:31–32

Seeking forgiveness: It is inevitable that when we do the work of healing, we often find areas in which we are bound to sin.

People are slaves to whatever has mastered them.
2 PETER 2:19

It may be an unconfessed sin from long ago or a habitual sin that we struggle with time and time again. In either case,

God calls us to seek forgiveness and accountability as part of the healing process.

> *Therefore confess your sins to each other and pray for each other so that you may be healed.*
> **JAMES 5:16**

BEAUTY FOR ASHES

Do you remember the diaries of our childhood with their tiny locks and keys? They almost served as a rite of passage for young girls, giving us permission to record and protect our secret thoughts and emotions. If you had one, you probably remember what it looked like and the sound the lock made when you turned the key. My Holly Hobby diary contained all the secrets of my twelve-year-old life—a list of cute boys, the pressures of middle school, my parents' divorce, arguments with siblings, and most importantly, the heartbreaking discovery that the boy I "loved" snacked on ants he picked off the brick school building, thereby destroying all hopes of ever having a boyfriend.

For many of us, our childhood diaries turned into lifelong journals that contained our greatest joys and deepest grief.

Several years after my divorce, I stood in my living room and held a dozen old journals in my arms. The weight of their contents far exceeded the weight of paper, and I no longer had the strength to carry them.

I was doing the active work of healing. I told myself the truth. I prayed and forgave. But the journals presented a problem. Over a decade of my life was inked upon their pages, serving as a permanent and visible record of my wounds. Some were leather journals, with pages *bound* together by string. Some were spiral notebooks, *bound* in wire. Others books, *bound* in glue. All the journals, however, remained *bound* by pain. I changed, but the journals did not. Every time I opened an old journal, I felt the cord around my neck pull me further to the ground, bending my back once again.

They had to go, and I reached out to a friend for help.

> *I will heal my people and will let them enjoy*
> *abundant peace and security.*
> **JEREMIAH 33:6**

Far outside of the city limits, I stood in my friend's backyard with the journals in my arms and a sweeping landscape before me. The city lights shone in the distance, competing with stars for my attention, but I fixed my eyes elsewhere. I knelt down in front of a rock-rimmed fire pit and laid my journals in the center, one by one. Memories bound by string, wire, and glue. Minutes, hours, days, and years of my life lay on the cold earth under a moonless night, and I struggled with the match to light the kindling.

I stood back and watched the fire take hold. At first, the flames preferred the crumpled newspaper and tiny branches, engulfing them in a fiery show of dominance. My journals, however, put up a fight, and the fire danced around their edges as it built strength and heat.

Crickets chirped their love songs in the distance as the fire grew. With the expanse of the land before me and the endless night above, I suddenly felt overcome by emotion. *I am so small in this world, and yet, You see me. You are with me, God.*

He raises the poor from the dust and lifts
the needy from the ash heap.
PSALM 113:7

I was not alone. The Unseen Companion stood beside me, and together we watched as the fire forced the cover of the first journal open. The ink-stained pages followed, dancing upright in the fiery wind as they blackened. The delicate pages of ash lingered for a moment before they broke into pieces and floated away.

As I watched the words of my life turn to ash before me, I felt a remarkable lightness, as though shackles and chains had fallen from my wrists and ankles. And with the cord around my neck untied, I drew in a deep breath and stood a bit straighter.

He has sent me to bind up the brokenhearted,
to proclaim freedom for the captives
and release from darkness for the prisoners . . .
to bestow on them a crown of beauty instead of ashes.
ISAIAH 61:1, 3

I distinctly remember watching one of the last pages burn. The edges turned black, and slowly the fire moved to the center of the page, leaving one word illuminated in the firelight. The word broke apart from the ash, untouched, and soared upward in the column of smoke, rising to heaven.

I often wonder what that one word was. Was it a word of complaint? Sorrow or anger? Was it a word of prayer or Scripture? If I were to guess which word rose to heaven fully intact, it would be "Peace."

*I will heal my people and will let them enjoy
abundant peace and security.*

JEREMIAH 33:6

HOMEBUILDING 101:
The Framework

HEALING

BUILDING YOUR HOME:

1. Go through the healing process outlined in the chapter to identify any ties you may need to break. This is not a quick or simple task, nor does it permanently remove the issue from your life. "Ties that bind" are powerful bondages that require purposeful work and often multiple acts of forgiveness, as Jesus described in Matthew 18:21–22.

- Identify an unwanted emotional response
- Follow the "ties that bind" backward to determine the trigger and original wounding
- Break the bondage with truth, prayer, and forgiveness
- Receive God's blessing

2. Do you or your children have any wounds that require the help of a counselor, doctor, or pastor? If so, develop a plan to obtain the help you need. Confide your intentions to someone close if you need accountability.

3. Do you struggle with helplessness or victimization due to unforgiveness? While dealing with this issue may evoke feelings of anger and resentment, it will empower you to create a healthy home and establish a new legacy for your children.

BUILDING A LEGACY OF FAITH: Model forgiveness

Let's be real. We make mistakes all the time in front of our children. We speak harshly to them, or perhaps they overhear us swear when we break a dish. At some point in our lives, our kids will likely witness a poor choice we made.

While we may admit our mistakes to one another, how difficult it is to seek forgiveness from our children. Many parents falsely assume they will lose authority and respect if they admit their mistake and ask for forgiveness. This is wholly untrue. Seeking forgiveness from our children helps them to establish a strong sense of stability and trust. It teaches them how to accept responsibility for their actions and make amends, when necessary. The frequent seeking and offering of forgiveness within a family sets the standard from which they will go before God with their failures.

Look for sincere opportunities to apologize and seek forgiveness from your child. Forgiveness has the power to transform both your home and legacy.

Strive for full restoration, encourage one another,
be of one mind, live in peace.
And the God of love and peace will be with you.
2 CORINTHIANS 13:11

CHAPTER 7

REST

When I am weary,
He is my Strength.

Journal Entry

I know You are with me, God, but I am just so physically tired and emotionally drained. Weary to the core of my soul. I no longer have the hope of getting everything done. I just try to get through each day, devoid of emotion that might sap me of what little energy I have.

In this state of exhaustion, emotion scares me the most. Dealing with my feelings right now is likened to playing with the torturous toy of childhood—the Jack-in-the-Box. I hated that clown. I remember turning the handle as a child, listening to the familiar and eerie tune, all the while preparing myself to jump in surprise. How often I set the Jack-in-the-Box on the shelf, just one note before it hit "POP!" Somehow, setting it aside seemed safer; although the next time I pulled it off the shelf, the wretched clown sat just beneath the surface, waiting to "POP" at the first turn of the handle.

THAT is how I feel emotionally right now. I keep my "handle" adjusted just so, with my emotions sitting just under the surface of my exhaustion, waiting for the opportune time to "POP" and show their ugly head. I can't afford a meltdown, God. I'm too tired. I don't have any reserve to deal with the tasks of daily life, much less my own stuff. What happens if I fall so hard, I can't recover? My girls need me, and I don't have the luxury to feel anything. I don't have the luxury to rest. And I am too tired to sleep. This weight of responsibility is too heavy for me to carry. Please, Lord. Give me strength for this day.

REST AND THE SINGLE MOTHER

Well-meaning but uninformed friends tried to offer comfort: "Remember, God won't give you more than you can handle." "Well, God must think I'm pretty strong," I replied with feigned stoicism. Outwardly I maintained composure, displaying the face of a strong Christian single mom who knew how to pull up her big-girl pants and get the job done. *After all, God thinks I can handle this.* Inside, however, I knew the crushing truth. I couldn't do it on my own. I was far weaker than what God and everyone else believed, and it was only a matter of time before everyone knew.

Can you relate to this level of exhaustion and weariness?

We press forward with our responsibilities and tasks of each day, without thought of our physical, emotional, or spiritual health. And many of us, believing that rest is a luxury, exhaust ourselves to the point of collapse.

Single moms, it is time to rest.

But before we can get to that, we must first clear up a few misperceptions. Many single mothers, in a valiant effort to care for their children and home, carry false beliefs about rest. See if any of the following misperceptions are familiar to you, and consider the blunt words of truth spoken by one who's been there.

I will rest when I finish the work. *We never finish the work. There is always another basket of laundry, another dish to wash. Rest.*

I don't have the luxury of resting. *Rest is not a luxury. It is a physical and emotional necessity. Rest.*

I don't have time to rest. *Resting, even for only a few minutes, will strengthen you to continue your work with greater efficiency and emotional stability. Your children will thank you. Rest.*

If I rest, everything will fall apart. *No, everything will wait patiently for you until after you have regained your strength. Trust me. Rest.*

If I rest, I will fall apart. *That just doesn't make sense. If you DON'T rest, you will fall apart. Rest.*

I will rest when I have help or get married. *Marriage is not an arrival. It is not a guarantee that everything will suddenly become easier. It is simply a different journey that carries new responsibilities. Rest, with or without help.*

Rest is a sign of laziness. *No, rest is a gift and requirement set forth by God. Even HE rested. Go REST. (Seriously, take a little power nap now or cuddle with your children and read to them. Put this book down and come back to it later.)*

The Unintentional, Guilt-Provoking Lie

My dear single moms—let me breathe a word of TRUTH into your life. I assume people have tried to console you with their favorite "scripture":

"Just remember, God isn't going to give you more than you can handle!"

How many times have you heard that expression? I heard

it more times than I care to remember, and not once did it offer a moment of comfort and strength. It only served as an empty platitude that fed my false belief that I was alone and was expected to handle things on my own. After hearing it, how could I rest? *My friends think I can handle this. God apparently knows I can handle this. Something must be terribly wrong with me because I SERIOUSLY CAN'T HANDLE THIS!*

I believed something was wrong with me.

Please feel free to scrap this belief. This common expression *sounds* like Scripture but is a false interpretation of God's Word. The original passage, in context, with emphasis added, is as follows:

> *No temptation has overtaken you except*
> *what is common to mankind.*
> *And God is faithful; <u>he will not let you be tempted</u>*
> <u>*beyond what you can bear.*</u>
> *But when you are tempted, he will also provide*
> *a way out so that you can endure it.*
> **1 CORINTHIANS 10:13**

This Scripture is speaking of *temptation*. You will not be *tempted beyond what you can bear.* In Paul's letter to the church of Corinth, he warns them to be on guard against falling into the sins of sexual immorality, idolatry, grumbling, and testing God. Nowhere in the context of the passage does it mention suffering or hardship.

Most single mothers carry far more than they can bear, with the belief that something must be wrong with them because they have grown weary. They wonder why they are not stronger. Wiser. More capable than they are. And like me, they worry about the day their life will fall apart, and everyone will discover how inadequate they are.

But here is the truth. *We live in a broken world.* As a result, marriages fail. Terrible things happen to good people. Accidents occur. Disease ravages bodies. Children die. Wars rage and people go hungry.

We suffer and grow weary, and at times the pressures will feel too much to bear. We are not strong enough to handle everything on our own. No one is.

If we maintained strength, wisdom, and righteousness on our own, why would we need a Savior?

We were under great pressure,
far beyond our ability to endure, so that we
despaired of life itself.
Indeed, we felt we had received the sentence of death.
But this happened that we might not rely on ourselves
but on God, who raises the dead.
2 CORINTHIANS 1:8–9

When my daughter suffered through multiple acts of self-harm, it was more than either of us could bear. When someone threatened our lives, it was more danger than I could withstand. When I woke up weary and exhausted, day after day as a single mother, it was more than I could carry on my own.

But with God all things are possible. He healed my daughter's wounds and gave her freedom from the bondage of self-harm. He protected our lives from violence, and He taught me to rest.

Jesus looked at them and said,
"With man this is impossible, but with God
all things are possible."
MATTHEW 19:26

The Invitation to Rest

Like a good parent, God models the behavior He would like to see in His children before giving a command. Our Father, the Creator of heaven and earth, *rested from His work.*

> *By the seventh day God had finished the work*
> *he had been doing;*
> *so on the seventh day he rested from all his work.*
> *Then God blessed the seventh day and made it holy,*
> *because on it he rested from all the work of*
> *creating that he had done.*
> **GENESIS 2:2-3**

God did not rest because He was tired. He rested from His work to set a precedent for His people. Knowing our propensity to strive and work despite our exhaustion, God gave us a Sabbath rest as a blessing and commanded it by law.

> *"There are six days when you may work,*
> *but the seventh day is a day of sabbath rest,*
> *a day of sacred assembly.*
> *You are not to do any work;*
> *wherever you live, it is a sabbath to the LORD."*
> **LEVITICUS 23:3**

When Jesus, the Son of God, dwelt on earth, He rested both as an example and out of need. Right before he met the woman at the well, Jesus sat down because He was tired and weary from traveling.

*Jacob's well was there, and Jesus, tired as he was from the
journey, sat down by the well.*

JOHN 4:6

We can take comfort knowing our Savior is not a distant
God, unsympathetic to our emotions, needs, and trials. Both
fully God and fully human, Jesus experienced exhaustion,
hunger, thirst, grief, anger, sadness, temptation, and longing
for His people. Jesus understands the human condition. When
his disciples returned from distant villages after anointing and
healing the sick, Jesus saw their weariness and offered them
rest *in His presence and care.*

*Then, because so many people were coming and going
that they did not even have a chance to eat, he said to them,
"Come with me by yourselves to a quiet place
and get some rest."*

MARK 6:31

Jesus invites us to lay down our endless striving, self-
imposed burdens, and societal expectations. He encourages us
to find our rest by taking on His yoke instead.

*"Come to me, all you who are weary and burdened,
and I will give you rest.
Take my yoke upon you and learn from me,
for I am gentle and humble in heart,
and you will find rest for your souls. For my yoke
is easy and my burden is light."*

MATTHEW 11:28-30

A yoke is a heavy, wooden bar, shaped to fit over the neck of two work animals. The yoke helps pairs of oxen, cattle, or horses to work as a team to pull a single plow or cart, and oftentimes, younger animals are placed with those who are experienced to help them learn. In this Scripture, Jesus offers to ease our burden by inviting us to come under His yoke of strength, guidance, teaching, service, and grace.

Through the yoke of Jesus, we share in His strength. No longer must we carry our burdens with a bent back, fearing the day our legs will falter beneath us. Rather, we remain confident in our weakness, knowing the power and might of Him who stands beside us.

> *But he said to me, "My grace is sufficient for you, for my*
> *power is made perfect in weakness." Therefore I will boast*
> *all the more gladly about my weaknesses,*
> *so that Christ's power may rest on me.*
> *That is why, for Christ's sake, I delight in*
> *weaknesses, in insults,*
> *in hardships, in persecutions, in difficulties.*
> *For when I am weak, then I am strong.*
> **2 CORINTHIANS 12:9-10**

Under His yoke, He gently leads us in the direction we should follow. No longer must we navigate our way through life, taking one uncertain step after another. Bound to Jesus, we walk shoulder to shoulder in the direction He chooses, all the while finding comfort in His companionship and security in His leading.

"For I know the plans I have for you," declares the LORD,
"plans to prosper you and not to harm you,
plans to give you hope and a future."
JEREMIAH 29:11

Taking His yoke upon our necks, we agree to submit to His loving authority and calling. No longer must we internally debate the choices before us, wondering if we should say this or do that. Just as Jesus only does what He sees His Father doing, we know what to do by watching Jesus work, speak, love, and serve.

Jesus gave them this answer:
"Very truly I tell you, the Son can do nothing by himself;
he can do only what he sees his Father doing,
because whatever the Father does the Son also does."
JOHN 5:19

"Now that I, your Lord and Teacher, have washed your feet,
you also should wash one another's feet.
I have set you an example that you should do
as I have done for you."
JOHN 13:14-15

"A new command I give you: Love one another.
As I have loved you, so you must love one another.
By this everyone will know that you are my disciples,
if you love one another."
JOHN 13:34-35

And in receiving the yoke of Jesus, we acknowledge He carried the scorn of our sin. No longer must we worry about our eternal home, for we know we will stand before our Father in heaven, clothed in the forgiveness and redemption of Jesus.

May he strengthen your hearts so that
you will be blameless and holy
in the presence of our God and Father when
our Lord Jesus comes with all his holy ones.
1 THESSALONIANS 3:13

RENEWED STRENGTH

Rest and strength are inherently connected. When we quiet ourselves and rest, we receive the refreshment and renewed strength of God.

"In repentance and rest is your salvation, in quietness and
trust is your strength . . ."
ISAIAH 30:15

We understand the physiological benefits of rest after exercise. Resting repairs the damage done to muscles, making them stronger than before. The same rule applies to the Sabbath rest. When we cease our work and rest in Jesus, we arise physically, emotionally, and spiritually stronger. Our mind and spirit soften to the will and Word of God. We are more likely to hear His gentle whispers or open our Bibles to receive His instruction. In a relaxed atmosphere, we are apt to engage in meaningful conversations with our children. And physically resting our bodies helps us to regain our strength for the work ahead.

He gives strength to the weary and increases
the power of the weak.
Even youths grow tired and weary, and young men
stumble and fall;

but those who hope in the LORD will renew their strength.
They will soar on wings like eagles; they will run
and not grow weary,
they will walk and not be faint.

ISAIAH 40:29-31

NAPTIME

I distinctly remember one occasion as a child when my mother laid me down to nap. In typical kid fashion, I fought and struggled as she pulled the covers over me. As I cried out, "But Mommy, I don't want to take a nap," she leaned in close, with eyebrows furrowed in exasperation.

"Michelle," she said. "There will come a day that you PRAY TO GOD FOR A NAP."

I continued to struggle, swearing I would never, ever pray to God for a nap. Oh, how I was wrong. Just as our mothers knew we needed to rest as a child, our Father in heaven knows we need to rest as an adult. What a gracious and loving God we have that He provided us with a Sabbath rest. Now we just need to settle down and choose to receive it.

The LORD is my shepherd; I shall not want. He makes
me lie down in green pastures.
He leads me beside still waters. He restores my soul.

PSALM 23:1-3 (ESV)

HOMEBUILDING 101:
The Framework

REST

BUILDING YOUR HOME:

1. What misperceptions do you have about rest?

2. Do you receive adequate rest each week (sleeping and purposeful time of relaxation)?

3. How might it change your family if you planned time to rest each week? How would it affect you personally?

4. Finding adequate time to rest is difficult for the single mother. Often, we only have a few moments to spare. Spending a few minutes each day in your "prayer closet" can provide a sense of rest and restored strength on even the busiest of days. A prayer closet is a place in your home that you regularly use for prayer.

"But when you pray, go into your room, close the door and pray to your Father, who is unseen. Then your Father, who sees what is done in secret, will reward you."

MATTHEW 6:6

BUILDING A LEGACY OF FAITH: Sleepytime Scriptures

When my oldest daughter, Rachel, was quite young, she had difficulty going to sleep. Once she did fall asleep, she often awoke with nightmares. I tried to comfort her with bedtime stories, songs, back rubs, and reassuring promises of safety. Nothing worked until I prayed God's Word over her. In a desperate search for answers, I searched my Bible for Scriptures about sleeping and found a verse that remains one of our favorites today.

I will lie down and sleep in peace,
for you alone, O LORD, make me dwell in safety.
PSALM 4:8 (NIV 1984)

Not only did I pray this Scripture over her for months, I wrote it on her pillowcase, which gave her a great sense of comfort. Eventually, Rachel memorized the verse and was able to use it to soothe herself to sleep.

Using simple Scriptures as part of a bedtime routine not only comforts and protects our children, it serves to build their foundation of faith that will last a lifetime.

When you lie down, you will not be afraid; when you lie
down, your sleep will be sweet.
PROVERBS 3:24

He will cover you with his feathers, and under
his wings you will find refuge;
his faithfulness will be your shield and rampart.
You will not fear the terror of night . . .
PSALM 91:4–5

PART FOUR

the
WALLS

"See, I have engraved you on the palms of my hands;
your walls are ever before me."
ISAIAH 49:16

CHAPTER 8

PROTECTION

When I am fearful,
He is my Protector.

L ast night, I scribbled a Bible verse on a scrap of paper and
tucked it under my pillow before going to sleep. Just having His Word within reach calmed my shaken heart. It was the
same verse I clung to, night after night, many years ago—
the same verse I wrote on the hem of my daughter's pillowcase
and whispered over her as we said our evening prayers.

I will lie down and sleep in peace,
for you alone, O LORD, make me dwell in safety.
PSALM 4:8 (NIV 1984)

I knew this chapter would be difficult to write, but I did
not anticipate the resurgence of fear that pumped through my
heart as I opened the twenty-three-year-old file folder yesterday. I thumbed through the paperwork, yellowed with age: police reports, copies of state statutes, written documentation and
timelines, Victim's Rights booklet, request for telephone trac-
ing equipment, gun purchase receipt, a newspaper article titled
"Living in Fear," a list of recommended safety precautions, and

various letters from the state Department of Criminal Investigation, and police and sheriff departments. I pulled the expired concealed-weapon permit from beneath a paper clip and studied the photo. My twenty-three-year-old self looked back at me with wary eyes, uncertain as to what her future would hold. *I was just a baby when I went through this . . .*

But I felt even more apprehensive reviewing the file *inside* the file. I kept copies of five letters hidden inside a second file folder to protect myself and others from seeing them unexpectedly. The folder sat unopened on my desk for hours yesterday before I found the courage to read them once again. I contemplated God's Word before I opened the file . . .

> *The LORD is on my side; I will not fear.*
> *What can man do to me?*
> **PSALM 118:6 (ESV)**

THE BIRTH OF FEAR

Married just under two years, my husband and I were both college students and had just returned home after spending Easter with my parents. I put my key up to the lock and realized the front door was already open. We looked at each other and questioned who forgot to lock up the house. But as we brought our luggage inside, we noticed things were out of place. Drawers opened. Papers scattered. Our wedding album sat on the coffee table, ripped into pieces.

Fear was born in that very heartbeat.

We soon found ourselves in a whirlwind of police activity as they combed through each room, asking questions and taking notes. The detectives dusted for fingerprints and classified the break-in as a stalking.

A few months later, threatening letters began to arrive, and by the time the phone calls started, my fear had grown into debilitating terror.

> *His eyes watch in secret for his victims; like a*
> *lion in cover he lies in wait.*
> *He lies in wait to catch the helpless; he catches the*
> *helpless and drags them off in his net.*
> **PSALM 10:8–9**

I didn't know who to be afraid of, so I became fearful of everyone. I stopped going to classes at the university and left the house only to go to work or the grocery store. I preferred staying in our home with all the lights on, curtains drawn, and the doors locked, chained, and deadbolted. Excruciating surges of fear caught me off guard. Sometimes, my body froze as adrenaline coursed through my veins, making it difficult to breathe. Other times, my hands uncontrollably shook as I journaled prayers, begging God for His protection. Only once did I find enough courage to lash out against my stalker during one of his breathing phone calls: "I don't think this is funny! I think you're sick!" I hung up and immediately regretted my impulsivity.

More letters arrived later that week. He knew I was pregnant.

THE FUNCTION OF FEAR

> *Even though I walk through the valley*
> *of the shadow of death,*
> *I will fear no evil, for you are with me;*
> *your rod and your staff, they comfort me.*
> **PSALM 23:4 (ESV)**

Hear my heart for a moment, single mothers. I had no desire to reawaken the memory of my stalking or to read the letters that first etched fear into my spirit. I had no intention of writing this chapter with trembling fingers and a racing pulse.

But some of you have gone through unimaginable circumstances, and would likely disregard empty words about God's protection. You long for an assurance that can only be offered by one who has been there.

I've known Fear—the kind of fear that loosens joints and weakens muscles, leaving me in an inconsolable heap on the floor. I've known a fear that brought out the protective momma within me, willing to fight to the death for my children. I've watched in fear as a loved one succumbed to drug and alcohol addiction, and I've crouched in fear during the onslaught of cruel words spoken over me.

> *I am in the midst of lions; I am forced to dwell*
> *among ravenous beasts—*
> *men whose teeth are spears and arrows, whose*
> *tongues are sharp swords.*
> **PSALM 57:4**

Unfortunately, I know many of you have experienced this level of fear and far worse. Some may even face the threat of danger in this moment. Please know I pray for the safety of you and your children. I also pray that as you read this chapter, you will find the hope and assurance of God's protection through His Word.

Most of you, however, have never undergone such terror and for that, I am grateful. But I also know you are not immune to debilitating fear. We've all known the deceptively small but pervasive fears that threaten to overtake one's life or at least a few minutes: fear of failure; fear of trying new things or meeting new people; fear of illness and injury and death; fear of losing your child, being alone, or marrying the wrong person; fear of confrontation, a spider, going outside, or checking your bank account balance. Know that I pray for you also—that you might find your courage and perseverance to keep fighting against that which inhibits you from moving forward.

Like many of you, I lived a life marked by fear.

But more importantly, I learned to live courageously within the protective arms of the Savior.

Have I not commanded you? Be strong and courageous.
Do not be afraid; do not be discouraged,
for the LORD your God will be with you wherever you go.
JOSHUA 1:9

Fear, in and of itself, is not a harmful emotion. It is an instinctual brain function designed to alert the body to danger and trigger a survival response. When we sense danger, whether real or imagined, physical or emotional, the brain pumps adrenaline and cortisol through our body. These stress hormones dilate our pupils and increase our heart rate, blood pressure, and blood sugars, thereby mobilizing us for a fight-or-flight response. Once the perceived threat has passed, our body functions slowly return to normal. Fear, in this capacity, serves as a God-given safety mechanism.

In contrast, prolonged fear associated with trauma, reoccurring threats, abusive relationships, or mental illness can have debilitating long-term consequences without the proper support. People who live in chronic fear may experience depression, anxiety disorders, sleep deprivation, eating and digestion issues, increased blood pressure, heart problems, headaches, and a decrease in cognitive functioning.

Like the poverty mindset, uncontrolled fear has the power to seep into our spirit, affecting not only our ability to engage in life but also our perception of God as our Protector. The apostle Paul speaks about the "spirit of fear" in a letter he wrote to encourage Timothy, a young man who served as Paul's companion and representative of the faith.

> *For God hath not given us the spirit of fear;*
> *but of power, and of love, and of a sound mind.*
> **2 TIMOTHY 1:7 (KJV)**

It is remarkable to consider that Paul wrote these words while chained and imprisoned under Emperor Nero. Having been beaten, stoned, and flogged, Paul had every reason to fear. Instead, he reminds us that we must reject the spirit of fear and embrace a spirit of power, love, and a sound mind—no matter what we may be going through.

IDENTIFICATION OF THE ENEMY

After I received the fourth letter from the stalker, things grew relatively quiet for a time. While I still lived with a spirit of fear, my response changed as I no longer retained the right to focus on myself. I now had an unborn child to protect, which emboldened me to seek out new strategies to deal with my fear.

Instead of hiding, I focused on safety precautions and the ability to defend my baby and myself. Combined with the strength found from the Book of Psalms, I mustered up enough courage to return to college and finish the semester in my ninth month of pregnancy.

My daughter was born on a cold day in January. I named her Rachel, meaning "little lamb." She symbolized all that was good and pure and beautiful in the world I now considered unsafe. Because the stalker still remained at large, I protected my daughter by embracing my newfound, momma-bear instinct and by claiming the powerful Word of God over her life.

He tends his flock like a shepherd:
He gathers the lambs in his arms and carries
them close to his heart;
he gently leads those that have young.
ISAIAH 40:11

Time passed uneventfully. My husband graduated, and his first job offer took us to a small town, hundreds of miles away. We moved without giving out our forwarding address and quickly settled into a quiet and anonymous life. Rachel grew into a beautiful toddler, and it seemed as if we had finally found our security.

Nearly three years after the initial break-in, I received the fifth and final letter.

The stalker's threats now focused on my daughter.

For our struggle is not against flesh and blood,
but against the rulers, against the authorities,
against the powers of this dark world
and against the spiritual forces of evil
in the heavenly realms.
EPHESIANS 6:12

I can't tell you what it was like to practice hiding with my toddler, silent and still, in a locked closet. Or how it felt to hold my child so tight, my heart started beating in time with hers. And I certainly can't describe the hopelessness I felt when I secretly made the decision to end my life if the threats against my daughter were carried out.

Sometimes, there are no words.

But, God and His Word remained.

And in Him, I found our strength and protection. In Him, I found my will to survive and embrace the life He graciously gave—no matter what the future held. I understood I may never learn the identity of my stalker or find closure or feel completely safe, but I stood in the shadow of my mighty Protector who knew the name and exact location of my enemy.

Have mercy on me, my God, have mercy on me,
for in you I take refuge.
I will take refuge in the shadow of your wings
until the disaster has passed.
PSALM 57:1

If I learned one great lesson from my experience, it is this: we have an enemy. Even as I did not know the identity of my stalker, we will never see this enemy face to face or know his full intent. But one thing is certain; he seeks to steal our abundance found in Jesus. In my experience, the enemy's greatest weapons against the single mother are poverty, loneliness, and fear. Understanding this helps us to find our courage as we take our stand against him.

Your enemy the devil prowls around like a roaring lion
looking for someone to devour.
Resist him, standing firm in the faith . . .
1 PETER 5:8-9

How We Respond to Fear

When I am afraid, I . . .

PSALM 56:3

It's been twenty years since the last letter from the stalker, and I still have not discovered the person's identity. After so long, one might expect me to be "over it" by now—that fear should no longer influence my life. I wish that was the case. Like many others who have suffered trauma, I must work to keep fear under control. Fear has loosened its grip around my throat, but it remains hidden in the shadows, waiting for an opportune time to make itself known. Fear shows up in quiet ways now, and, at times, I don't even realize my responses to life are fear-based.

Perhaps you struggle with the same issues.

I need to speak with someone about an important issue but choose to remain silent—in fear of a verbal attack. I allow a new opportunity to slip through my fingers, refusing even to give it a chance—in fear of failure. I own enough art supplies to equip a professional studio, yet I fail to place the canvas on the easel—in fear of making a mistake. I refuse to put on a swimming suit and feel the summer sun and water on my skin—in fear of ridicule. And as I write this book, I stare at the blank computer screen, day after day, month after month, with words caught in my throat—in fear that my story is not worth telling.

The enemy's use of fear is pervasive, cunning, and cruel. Even after the threat of perceived danger has passed, he uses our residual fear to steal the abundant life we have in Jesus.

But if we understand the ways of the enemy, our typical responses to fear, and the power of God's Word, we can face our fears in full assurance of our Savior's love and protection.

Below is a list of the common responses to fear, no matter how large or small the perceived threat. Our "immediate physical response" is usually an involuntary reaction and is neither good nor bad. While the behaviors associated with the "spirit of fear" are normal for those who have undergone trauma, they can become detrimental and debilitating long-term if not dealt with. And when dealing with fear, responding with Scripture is always a powerful choice as the Holy Spirit intercedes with protection, wisdom, and discernment in our time of need.

Fight

- Immediate physical response: physical or verbal defense of self and children.
- Long-term, "spirit of fear" response: bitterness, jealousy, suspicion, cynicism, anger, or rage.
- Biblical response: fight spiritually. *"Praise be to the LORD my Rock, who trains my hands for war, my fingers for battle"* (Ps. 144:1).

"Finally, be strong in the Lord and in his mighty power. Put on the full armor of God, so that you can take your stand against the devil's schemes. For our struggle is not against flesh and blood, but against the rulers, against the authorities, against the powers of this dark world and against the spiritual forces of evil in the heavenly realms. Therefore put on the full armor of God, so that when the day of evil comes, you may be able to stand your ground, and after you have done everything, to stand. Stand firm then, with the belt of truth buckled around your waist, with the breastplate of righteousness in place, and with your feet fitted with the readiness that comes from the gospel of peace. In addition

*to all this, take up the shield of faith, with which you can
extinguish all the flaming arrows of the evil one. Take the
helmet of salvation and the sword of the Spirit, which is the
word of God. And pray in the Spirit on all occasions with
all kinds of prayers and requests. With this in mind, be alert
and always keep on praying for all the Lord's people.*
EPHESIANS 6:10-18

Flight

- Immediate physical response: Run away. Hide.
- Purposeful, healthy response: Seek safety and shelter for self and children. Leave abuser.
- Long-term, "spirit of fear" response: Disengage with life. Isolate. Withdraw. Engage in activities that distract or numb feelings. Develop addictions.
- Biblical response: Find your hiding place in God. *You are my hiding place; you will protect me from trouble and surround me with songs of deliverance* (Ps. 32:7).

Fright

- Immediate physical response: Inability to move or speak. Temporary paralysis.
- Long-term, "spirit of fear" response: Inability to make choices or confront issues. Ignore problems. Remain "stuck" in harmful relationships and environments.
- Biblical response: Find courage in His presence. *"Be strong and courageous. Do not be afraid or terrified because of them, for the LORD your God goes with you; he will never leave you nor forsake you"* (Deut. 31:6).

Succumb

- Immediate physical response: Body goes limp. Offer no resistance.
- Long-term, "spirit of fear" response: Give up. Resign self to a life of misery. Give in to temptations. Cease dreaming and striving for a better life. Develop victim mentality. In extreme cases, may have suicidal thoughts.
- Biblical response: Persevere. *"Be on your guard; stand firm in the faith; be courageous; be strong"* (1 Cor. 16:13).

Seek Help

- Immediate physical response: Yell. Call out for help.
- Purposeful, healthy response: Involve the police. Obtain counseling, pastoral care, and legal assistance. Develop a strong support system.
- Long-term, "spirit of fear" response: Expect others (family, friends, men) to continually rescue.
- Biblical response: Call upon the mighty name of God. *"And everyone who calls on the name of the LORD will be saved"* (Joel 2:32).

DEEPER TRUST

The majority of God's protection goes largely unnoticed. It remains hidden behind the thin veil between what is seen and unseen. But every once in a while, God's hand of protection is remarkably visible.

Five years after I became a single mother, someone broke into our home while we were away. They entered through a window and unlocked all the windows of the house before leaving. The police classified the incident as a "stalking" but could not connect the two cases. They warned me the intruder probably intended to return.

Although it had been eleven years since the last letter from the stalker, this new threat pushed me into a place of fear I had not yet known. *I was on my own with the girls—their only protector.* I questioned my ability to keep my daughters from harm. I worried I would not hear an intruder enter my house or that we would be caught by surprise. I was afraid to sleep or to have the television volume too loud. Refusing to succumb to this resurrected spirit of fear, I asked God for help and trusted in His Word and promise of protection.

> *The LORD is my strength and my shield; my heart*
> *trusts in him, and he helps me.*
> **PSALM 28:7**

While the girls and I remained protected behind the invisible hand of God, He graciously calmed my fears by also providing a *visible* shield of protection. Her name was Liesl, a 120-pound German shepherd with a pedigree boasting generations of advanced *Schutzhund* titles, elite certifications that focus on tracking, obedience, and protection. As loving and beautiful as she was protective, Liesl served as a fierce defender and faithful companion to the girls and me.

When we took Liesl for a walk around the neighborhood, people crossed the street to avoid being in close proximity. When someone came to the door, she barked with such force that I often had to convince visitors it was safe for them to enter. And while we slept, I felt certain she rested with one eye open. For eight years, I never feared for our physical safety, and there were times I entertained the idea she might be an angel in disguise.

Last September, Liesl became ill, and I made the decision no dog owner wants to face. While my heart was utterly broken, I understood she had fulfilled her duty to God and my family. Now, it was her turn to rest. We had a daylong goodbye, filled with all of her favorites: a short walk, belly rubs, whispers of thanks, whipped cream in a can, and as many marshmallows as she wanted.

Since I lost Liesl, God has called me into a deeper level of trust. I can no longer put my confidence in the eyes, ears, and bite of my dog. Instead, I must put my confidence in the eyes, ears, and capable hand of God, my Unseen Protector. I still feel the temptation to fear, but I no longer live with the spirit of fear.

> *Say to those with fearful hearts,*
> *"Be strong, do not fear; your God will come,*
> *he will come with vengeance;*
> *with divine retribution he will come to save you."*
> **ISAIAH 35:4**

HOPE IN THE MIDST OF SUFFERING

Having worked in single-mother ministries for many years, I know this chapter has likely been difficult for many of you. I've heard your stories. I've prayed with you and cried with you. And as I write about God's protection, I know the gnawing issue many of you are wrestling with now.

But God didn't protect me! Where was He? Why didn't He protect my children or save my marriage? If He is so mighty, so powerful and good, why does He allow such evil in the world?

I can't tell you how many times I've uttered those exact

words to God through tears and clenched teeth. They are the same questions the world has wrestled with since the dawn of time and the same questions that fuel the unbeliever.

My God, my God, why have you forsaken me?
Why are you so far from saving me, so far from
my cries of anguish?
PSALM 22:1

While I've come to trust God in the areas I don't fully understand, I struggle in this moment to find the right words to offer you hope. But as I muddle through—hear my heart, single mothers. God loves you. He sees you and hears you. He was with you during your darkest moments and will continue to be with you as you move forward. Your suffering does not indicate His lack of presence, love, or concern, nor is it a form of punishment.

Contrary to popular opinion, God has not promised us an easy life if we endeavor to follow Him. Instead, He promises us *eternal life* through the power of Jesus' work on the cross. He has not promised a life free from pain, trial, and suffering; rather, we know there will be hardship and sorrow. Consider the words of the apostle Peter:

Dear friends, do not be surprised at the fiery
ordeal that has come on you to test you,
as though something strange were happening to you.
But rejoice inasmuch as you participate in
the sufferings of Christ,
so that you may be overjoyed when his glory is revealed.
1 PETER 4:12-13

Our God, in His infinite love and wisdom, gave us a tremendous gift: free choice. He is not a tyrant who forces allegiance or obedience. He is not a puppet master. He's given us the freedom to choose or reject His love, forgiveness, and redemption.

And as a result, we live in an irreparably broken world in which humans sin and humans suffer. And some of us suffer greatly.

But God promises restoration. While the world continues on its path of destruction, God transforms what the enemy intended for evil and uses it for our good.

And we know that in all things God works for
the good of those who love him,
who have been called according to his purpose.
ROMANS 8:28

This is where we find hope in the midst of suffering. Our gracious God does not allow anything to go to waste, but works continually to redeem our story. It is through the experience of darkness that we learn to value the Light. We better understand the true magnitude and beauty of the mountain after we've experienced the depths of the valley. And it is through His redemption that you now hold this book in your hands.

Nothing is lost on God. Not even my story.

We will encounter suffering in this world. Yet we have nothing to fear. We stand firm in the knowledge that nothing can separate us from the love of Christ, and in this hope we find the courage to persevere.

For I am convinced that neither death nor life,
neither angels nor demons,

neither the present nor the future, nor any powers,
neither height nor depth, nor anything else in all creation,
will be able to separate us from the love of God that is in
Christ Jesus our Lord.

ROMANS 8:38-39

So do not fear, single momma. Be courageous. Your story is one of redemption.

When you are afraid, God is your Unseen Protector.

When you need to flee, God is your Hiding Place.

When you must fight, God will equip you.

When you feel like giving up, God will strengthen you.

When you must move forward, you will find your courage in His presence.

And when the spirit of fear rises within you, the love of Jesus will drive it out.

There is no fear in love. But perfect love drives out fear . . .

1 JOHN 4:18

HOMEBUILDING 101:
The Longing for Home

PROTECTION

BUILDING YOUR HOME:

1. When have you felt physically, emotionally, or spiritually unsafe? Are you physically and emotionally safe now?*

2. When you feel unsafe, how do you respond? Refer to the chapter section detailing typical responses to fear, if needed.

3. What perceptions do you have about God's ability and willingness to protect you and your children?

4. What Scriptures evoke the strongest feelings of comfort, security, protection, and peace? For assistance, refer to *Building on Solid Ground: "Scriptures for the Single Mother"* on page 213.

* NOTE: If you are currently in danger or live with uncontrollable fear or anxiety, seek professional help from a counselor, pastor, or law enforcement agency.

BUILDING A LEGACY OF FAITH: Trust your children to God
Because my daughter's life began in extreme danger, I found it

virtually impossible to trust my children to anyone—including God. I felt the need to control every aspect of their lives to ensure their safety. Eventually, I entrusted my daughters to God as I learned His love for them and protection over them far exceeded my own. Consider the following verses as you learn to put your children in the hands of God each day.

God values His children.

People were bringing little children to Jesus
for him to place his hands on them,
but the disciples rebuked them. When Jesus saw this,
he was indignant.
He said to them, "Let the little children come to me,
and do not hinder them,
for the kingdom of God belongs to such as these.
Truly I tell you, anyone who will not receive the kingdom
of God like a little child
will never enter it." And he took the children in his arms,
placed his hands on them and blessed them.

MARK 10:13-16

God does not tolerate evil against His children.

"If anyone causes one of these little ones—those who
believe in me—to stumble,
it would be better for them to have a large millstone
hung around their neck
and to be drowned in the depths of the sea."

MATTHEW 18:6

The angels of children hold a high rank in heaven and see the face of God.

"See that you do not despise one of these little ones.
For I tell you that their angels in heaven always see
the face of my Father in heaven."
MATTHEW 18:10

God reveals His wonders to His children.

At that time Jesus said,
"I praise you, Father, Lord of heaven and earth,
because you have hidden these things from
the wise and learned,
and revealed them to little children."
MATTHEW 11:25

Through the praise of children and infants
you have established a stronghold against your enemies,
to silence the foe and the avenger.
PSALM 8:2

CHAPTER 9

PEACE

When I am worried,
He is my Peace.

Many years ago, I taught in a three-room schoolhouse in the Wyoming mountains. The pride and joy of this tiny community was its one store, which offered groceries, an assortment of home décor and kitchenware, and a critically acclaimed café, nationally known for its gourmet fare.

While waiting in the café for dinner one evening, my gaze once again found the stained-glass lamps scattered throughout the store. I adored those lamps and dreamed of the day I could afford to buy one. Their jewel-toned light cast warmth reminiscent of the home in my imagination—a home filled with music, books, love, laughter, and only kind words.

When I could no longer endure the wait, I purchased a lamp and brought my stained-glass treasure home where it belonged. For several years, my beloved lamp cast its warm glow in an otherwise cold house. And after my divorce, the lamp served as a gentle reminder of the home I aspired to create.

But as tends to happen in every family with young children, the lamp broke after a series of little-girl tumbles, twirls, and jumps. Rachel cried in genuine remorse and tried to pick up the pieces. I pulled her close and removed the broken glass from her hands, assuring her all was well. The lamp could be repaired. She immediately brightened and ran to take care of her little sister while I cleaned up the mess.

My heart shifted toward my lamp. I held the shards of glass tight in my hands, as if my love and sorrow alone had the power to mend what was broken.

I held much of my life that way—especially worry. *Am I doing enough? Will the money last? What if I lose my job? Am I parenting the girls well?*

I held worry like broken shards of glass—somehow believing I could mend all that was broken through my love and sorrow. I could mend if I held on tight enough. I carried the regret of yesterday, the concerns of today, and the anxiety about tomorrow with a sense of sacrificial obligation, believing I would find solutions if I thoroughly analyzed all the potential outcomes. And when I was feeling particularly gracious and responsible, I even picked up the illegitimate worries of others and held them as my own.

Who of you by worrying can add a single hour to your life?
LUKE 12:25

When it came to my lamp, I understood I did not have the ability to fix it myself. I trusted it to an expert, who repaired the lamp with artistry and precision. Although a few scars remain, the repair surprisingly improved the lamp, making it stronger than when it was new.

Yet, it would take years before I could entrust my worry to God, and quite honestly, I still struggle from time to time.

I suspect you hold broken shards of worry, as well. After all, isn't it the duty and moral obligation of every single mother to worry incessantly?

The truth is, when we lie awake in bed at 2:00 a.m. with a hundred-pound weight on our chest and shards of glass clenched in our bloody fists, it's far from an act of responsibility. It's downright dangerous—physically, emotionally, and spiritually. It's time we unclench our fists and release what is not ours to carry.

Letting Go of Worry and Anxiety

—to bestow on them a crown of beauty instead of ashes,
the oil of joy instead of mourning,
and a garment of praise instead of a spirit of despair.
ISAIAH 61:3

God's most lavish gifts require a trade. This is not to say that we must purchase or earn His blessings. No. But if we wish to receive His gifts in full measure, we must first empty our hands of all that hinders us. We give Him our ashes in exchange for a crown of beauty, our poverty for His abundance, and our weakness for His strength. Jesus bore our sin unto death on the cross that we might have life.

Following a pattern similar to David's Psalms of lament, the apostle Paul teaches us how to cast aside our worry in exchange for God's peace:

Do not be anxious about anything, but in every situation,
by prayer and petition, with thanksgiving,
present your requests to God.
And the peace of God, which transcends all understanding,
will guard your hearts and your minds in Christ Jesus.
PHILIPPIANS 4:6-7

1. *Do not be anxious about anything.* The word *anxious* derives from the Greek word *merimnaó,* which means "to be divided, distracted, or to go to pieces." How often do we "go to pieces" under the stress and weight of anxiety? How often do we allow worry to tear at the fabric of our soul and tempt us to remain stuck in the well-worn rut of fear and doubt? Take heart. The enduring and all-encompassing love of God allows us to approach His throne with confidence to cast our burdens on Him.

Cast your cares on the LORD and he will sustain you;
he will never let the righteous be shaken.
PSALM 55:22

Cast all your anxiety on him because he cares for you.
1 PETER 5:7

Consider the wording of these Scriptures. We are not instructed to lay our anxiety down gently before the Lord. This is not the "quiet passing of the offering plate at church" kind of sacrifice. Rather, we are told to *cast* our anxiety on Him. The Hebrew and Greek wording for "cast" means to throw, fling, or hurl. To *cast* our burdens on the Lord requires purposeful and powerful movement. Think of a baseball pitcher who takes his stance, focuses his eyes where he wants the ball to go, and uses his body's momentum to throw the ball with velocity. We *cast* our worry on God—our regrets and shame, our what ifs and should haves, our fears and anxiety—*because He cares for us.* Just as I didn't want my daughter to pick up the broken shards of glass, God does not want us to carry what is harmful.

2. . . . *in every situation, by prayer and petition, with thanksgiving, present your requests to God.* Once we have cast our anxieties on God, we make our requests through prayer, petition, and thanksgiving. "Petition" implies a specific request stemming from a deeply personal, urgent, or felt need. In other words, we transform our worry into a prayer request and submit it to God with a heart of thanks.

3. *And the peace of God, which transcends all understanding, will guard your hearts and your minds in Christ Jesus.* God does not promise to answer our prayers exactly as we requested, nor does He guarantee us freedom from hardship.

> *"I have told you these things, so that in me*
> *you may have peace.*
> *In this world you will have trouble. But take heart!*
> *I have overcome the world."*
> **JOHN 16:33**

Rather, He gives us a *peace that transcends all understanding,* which will protect our hearts and minds *in Christ Jesus.* In exchange for our *anxiety,* He offers a *peace* found *in Jesus.* Taken from the Greek word *eiréné,* "peace" means "to join or tie together in a whole." In essence, when life's hardships, sufferings, and trials pull us to pieces (anxiety—*merimnaó*), Jesus gives us inner-wholeness (peace—*eiréné*) by mending what was once broken.

> *He has sent me to bind up the brokenhearted . . .*
> **ISAIAH 61:1**

This unmistakable peace of Jesus serves as a nourishing and healing balm against this hurting world, allowing us to endure and even thrive under hardship. It enables us to weep with hope, suffer with love, and die with joy.

REMAINING IN PEACE

You will keep in perfect peace those whose minds are stead-fast, because they trust in you.
ISAIAH 26:3

It is a familiar pattern now, almost laughable in its predict-ability. Once I've received God's peace, it is nearly impossible for me to hold on to it. I'm now quite adept at casting my worry and anxiety on God and receiving His peace in return. All is calm within my unburdened heart as I rest in Him—for a moment or two.

The trick is learning how to *remain* in His peace. While skilled at "casting my anxiety," I have yet to master the art of fully letting go. I continually return to the foot of the cross—not to stand within its shadow of grace and peace, but to reclaim what is no longer mine to carry. I stoop to pick up the discarded fragments of fear, worry, and anxiety. I piece to-gether the broken shards of insecurity and doubt. I would venture to guess I'm not the only one.

Long before modern psychology, the apostle Paul recog-nized the powerful influence our thoughts have over our emo-tional and spiritual wellbeing.

The mind governed by the flesh is death, but the mind governed by the Spirit is life and peace.
ROMANS 8:6

Do not conform to the pattern of this world, but be trans-formed by the renewing of your mind.
ROMANS 12:2

We demolish arguments and every pretension that sets itself
up against the knowledge of God, and we take captive every
thought to make it obedient to Christ.
2 CORINTHIANS 10:5

Paul also understood it was not enough to cast our anxiety on God. To remain in God's peace, we must exchange anxious thoughts for messages of truth and wisdom. Today, psychologists call this "thought replacement," a technique used in cognitive behavioral therapy, in which patients replace destructive and negative thought patterns with healthy thoughts and visualizations.

Do not be anxious about anything, but in every situation,
by prayer and petition, with thanksgiving,
present your requests to God.
And the peace of God, which transcends all understanding,
will guard your hearts and your minds in Christ Jesus.
Finally, brothers and sisters, whatever is true,
whatever is noble,
whatever is right, whatever is pure, whatever is lovely,
whatever is admirable—
if anything is excellent or praiseworthy—think
about such things.
PHILIPPIANS 4:6-8

Immediately after casting our anxiety on God and receiving His peace, we are called to think about truth, nobility, and righteousness. Most things of this world fall vastly short of such virtue. For who is true, noble, right, pure, lovely, admirable, excellent, and praiseworthy other than Jesus? Only He possesses such qualities in full measure. When we focus on the character of Jesus, it allows us to view ourselves, others, and our circumstances through the lens of grace and mercy, which protects us against the return of anxious thoughts that consume our strength and spirit.

> *Set your minds on things that are above,*
> *not on things that are on earth.*
> **COLOSSIANS 3:2 (ESV)**

Even as I write in this moment, a specific worry rises to my attention and consumes my thoughts. It is not baseless anxiety, but one borne of genuine concern and threat—one I have struggled with for a couple of months now. How quickly it moves to the forefront of my mind and distracts me from all that is good and right.

And so the process begins again.

1. Cast my anxiety on God. *It is nearly August, and I still haven't secured a teaching position for this coming year. What if I can't find anything? How will I pay my bills? What will happen to our family? Oh, Lord—I cast my worry on You. I can't carry this on my own, or it will consume me.*

2. Present my request to Him with prayer, petition, and thanksgiving. *Please help me find employment so I can help provide for my family. You know our needs and where I can best serve as a teacher. Thank you for walking with me through this. I know You will never leave or abandon me.*

3. Receive God's peace, which transcends all understanding. *(Deep breath. Rest.)*

4. Shift my focus back on what is true, noble, right, pure, lovely, admirable, excellent, and praiseworthy. *Lord, I am reminded of your Word—"For I know the plans I have for you,' declares the LORD, 'plans to prosper you and not to harm you, plans to*

give you hope and a future'" (Jer. 29:11). *You are truly loving and faithful, and I trust myself to You. Amen.*

Broken Made Whole

Just before Gabrielle turned nine years old, she informed me she didn't want the typical party and presents for her birthday. "I want to use that money to go on a vacation with you and Rachel instead," she said. "I've never even been to a hotel with you." She added her pretend pout for good measure and ran outside to play with the neighbor boys. While Gabrielle's birthday wish exuded sweetness and generosity, she obviously didn't understand the financial pressure I carried. Once again, I added shards of glass to my ever-increasing collection of worry. In one hand, I held the worry about how much a vacation would cost. In the other, I held the worry that I had not instilled a sense of joy and adventure in my daughters. Other than our camping disaster and a few trips to visit family, we had not had the opportunity to go on a real vacation.

After a bit of research, I learned that the YMCA of the Rockies, just above Estes Park, Colorado, offered an exceptionally affordable, all-inclusive weekend package for families. If I shifted my budget and included Gabrielle's monetary birthday gift from my parents, we could afford to go.

A few weeks later, we found ourselves surrounded by the snow-capped Rocky Mountains, brimming with fragrant pines and aspen trees whose yellowed leaves danced in the autumn breeze. In addition to hiking and exploring, the family package included roller-skating, campfires, marshmallow roasts, hayrides, and a kid-friendly dance. We relished every moment of our vacation, and Gabrielle took particular pride in choosing such a fine gift. But God soon revealed a greater purpose in bringing us to the mountains.

> *"Peace I leave with you; my peace I give you.*
> *I do not give to you as the world gives.*
> *Do not let your hearts be troubled and do not be afraid."*
> **JOHN 14:27**

While exploring the grounds of the YMCA, the girls and I discovered the Mootz Family Craft and Design Center, which offered dozens of self-guided art projects, including woodworking, leather stamping, ceramic painting, and jewelry making. Being artsy in nature, we quickly settled into one of the more challenging projects—glass mosaics. We each picked a wooden shape and chose our glass from bins filled with broken shards in all colors, textures, shapes, and sizes. Once we found a color we liked, we dug a metal scoop into the bin to safely remove the glass and pour it onto our supply tray.

As we started piecing together our mosaics, I felt the Holy Spirit's presence, gently nudging me into a deeper understanding of what God was doing with our lives. I watched my girls work side by side, as they painstakingly glued shards of glass onto their wooden forms. Occasionally, Gabrielle whispered something, and in response, Rachel would pick up a glass cutter and shape a piece to just the right size for her little sister. All was quiet and peaceful and good, allowing me to breathe deeply for the first time in years.

I dug a scoop into a bin of brightly colored glass and poured the contents into my hand, feeling the sharp edges push into my skin. As I studied and sorted through the pieces, I remembered my stained-glass lamp and finally understood the weight of worry I had carried for years.

I held my *family* like broken shards of glass in my hands.

I was unable to mend what had shattered in our lives and was unwilling to let go of what was precious. And so, for years I wrapped my fingers tightly around our broken pieces and held them with both love and sorrow. *We might be broken, but at least we're together.*

But in that craft center, we took what was broken to create something new. *Perhaps that is what God was doing in our lives.*

In that moment of realization, a great conversation began that continued in the days, months, and years ahead. As the girls and I created our beautiful mosaics from what was once broken, the Holy Spirit whispered in my ear, reminding me of the Word of God, already embedded in my heart.

Lord, I don't know how to heal my broken family . . .

He heals the brokenhearted and binds up their wounds.
PSALM 147:3

But, I've made so many mistakes . . .

The LORD is compassionate and gracious,
slow to anger, abounding in love.
PSALM 103:8

When I think of all that we have gone through . . .

"Forget the former things; do not dwell on the past.
See, I am doing a new thing!
Now it springs up; do you not perceive it?"
ISAIAH 43:18-19

And all we have lost . . .

[He has sent me]
to bestow on them a crown of beauty instead of ashes,
the oil of joy instead of mourning,
and a garment of praise instead of a spirit of despair.
ISAIAH 61:3

It is difficult to not want to give up . . .

"But as for you, be strong and do not give up,
for your work will be rewarded."
2 CHRONICLES 15:7

Most of the time, I feel alone and afraid . . .

"So do not fear, for I am with you;
do not be dismayed, for I am your God.
I will strengthen you and help you;
I will uphold you with my righteous right hand."
ISAIAH 41:10

And sometimes I don't know what to do, what choices to
make, or what direction to follow . . .

I will instruct you and teach you in the way you should go;
I will counsel you with my loving eye on you.
PSALM 32:8

Whether you turn to the right or to the left,
your ears will hear a voice behind you, saying,
"This is the way; walk in it."
ISAIAH 30:21

My heart breaks for my girls who want a father in the home ...

> *A father to the fatherless, a defender of widows,*
> *is God in his holy dwelling.*
> **PSALM 68:5**

But how will You Father them?

> *He tends his flock like a shepherd:*
> *He gathers the lambs in his arms and carries*
> *them close to his heart;*
> *he gently leads those that have young.*
> **ISAIAH 40:11**

Oh, Lord, my mind returns quickly to worry as there is still so much to do and think about. I don't even know where to begin ...

> *"Be still, and know that I am God."*
> **PSALM 46:10**

Be still, single mommas.

Know God will take your worry and anxiety—all that is shattered and broken—and transform it into something whole and beautiful. Stronger than before. You simply need to let go of what is not yours to carry.

> *Wait for the LORD; be strong and take heart*
> *and wait for the LORD.*
> **PSALM 27:14**

HOMEBUILDING 101:
The Walls

PEACE

BUILDING YOUR HOME:

1. Do you consider yourself a worrier? What circumstances or issues provoke the greatest amount of worry and anxiety?

2. Practice letting go of worry, using Philippians 4:6–8 as a guideline.

Let go of your anxiety by transforming it into a request to God.

Do not be anxious about anything, but in every situation,
by prayer and petition, with thanksgiving,
present your requests to God.

Receive His peace.

And the peace of God, which transcends all understanding,
will guard your hearts and your minds in Christ Jesus.

Shift your focus.

Finally, brothers and sisters, whatever is true,
whatever is noble,
whatever is right, whatever is pure, whatever is lovely,
whatever is admirable—
if anything is excellent or praiseworthy—think
about such things.

BUILDING A LEGACY OF FAITH: Model the use of God's Word
As a single mom and the spiritual head of your household, it is imperative to not only teach your children about God's Word, but also to model how to use Scripture as a source of direction, strength, and hope. When your children have a particular issue they are dealing with, show them how to search for an answer in the Bible using the concordance. Online Bibles provide powerful search tools that simplify this process, in addition to other resources that aid in the understanding of Scripture.

On occasion, I also model this process to my children by sharing a personal issue. This allows them to see the effectiveness God's Word has on my life. I only share minor issues that will not threaten their sense of safety or security. For example, I might express my unhappiness in needing to clean the house: "I am too tired, and the house is too messy. It's too hard, and I don't have the strength. I wonder what God might say about that . . ."

Using "strength" as a keyword, I could then find and share an appropriate Scripture that encourages me to do my job.

I can do all this through him who gives me strength.
PHILIPPIANS 4:13

Not realizing the powerful influence this modeling had on my daughters, I was shocked to receive an encouraging and timely Scripture from my daughter Gabrielle. She knew I felt nervous to sing a solo for a church Christmas event. As I took my place on the stage and opened my music folder, I noticed the following Scripture scrawled in seven-year-old handwriting on my music.

> *Don't be afraid, for I am with you.*
> *Don't be discouraged, for I am your God.*
> *I will strengthen you and help you.*
> *I will hold you up with my victorious right hand.*
> **ISAIAH 41:10 (NLT)**

PART FIVE

the

ROOF

And over all these virtues put on love, which
binds them all together in perfect unity.
COLOSSIANS 3:14

CHAPTER 10

LOVE

When I long for love,
He is my Beloved.

Tears fell, heavy and silent, as I drove home, bathing my face in repentant sorrow. *Why, Lord? Why did I do this? I didn't intend for this to happen!*

> *For I do not understand my own actions.*
> *For I do not do what I want, but I do the very thing I hate.*
> **ROMANS 7:15 (ESV)**

I just wanted to wash the shame from my body as quickly as possible—not because anything was taken from me, but because I willingly gave myself away in exchange for counterfeit love. *I knew better.* I wanted to hold my daughters close and cling instead to what was right and holy and blessed.

When I arrived home, I rushed to the bathroom and scrubbed the remnants of lipstick and mascara from my face. A shell of a woman stood in the mirror, and for a moment, I didn't recognize her. She seemed a stranger to the virtuous woman I once dreamed of becoming.

"Although you wash yourself with soap
and use an abundance of cleansing powder,
the stain of your guilt is still before me,"
declares the Sovereign LORD.
JEREMIAH 2:22

After I collected myself, I tucked my girls into bed, and with the same lips that kissed a man I would never see again, I kissed my daughters goodnight and whispered words of love into their ears.

A JOURNAL ENTRY

Oh, Lord.

Why am I so willing to succumb to less than Your will for my life? Am I so starving for affection that I am willing to eat the crumbs that fall from the table? Love is not yet mine to hold and nevertheless, I was willing to accept a crude mirage. Why is it so difficult for me to realize I am worth far more than what I accept? I am worth the time it takes to pursue. I am worth the endless conversations. I am worth being looked in the eye and told, "I love you." I am worth a commitment made before You and my loved ones. And my daughters—they are worth infinitely more than what they've been given.

WHY then, do I settle for less? Out of desperation? Longing?

Longing is perhaps our greatest burden and deepest suffering as a family right now.

I long for touch, companionship, and a chest to rest my weary head upon. Loneliness wells from within the deepest caverns of my soul, flooding my heart, mind, and body with desire. I long to love again and be loved in return.

My girls long for a fatherly voice, assuring them all is well. They long for strong arms to catch them when they fall and carry them when they are weak.

But, longing and need are two different things.

I long for a husband, but I NEED You, Lord. My daughters long for a father figure, but they NEED You. We need Your grace and love as our Savior. We need Your guidance and protection as our heavenly Father. I imagine us wrapped in Your arms now— protected, cherished, and loved like a father holds his children.

Oh, Lord, forgive me! Cover me with your love and show me You are enough in our time of waiting. Seal up this heart of mine once again, and draw me back within Your will. Help me to lead my daughters on a path of righteousness by more than words. Let me lead by example.

Amen.

HEARTSICK

Hope deferred makes the heart sick,
but a longing fulfilled is a tree of life.
PROVERBS 13:12

And in this moment, single momma, you and I shift from new friends to old friends. It is a painful experience to place one's life, in all its rawness and shame, on display for the world to see. In fact, I had a little argument with God about this chapter, believing it was unnecessary to divulge intimate details of my dating history. *But, God, people will judge. I don't like this part of my history. Can't we just skip to the part about Your love?*

Despite the emotional plea, my fingers continued to type in obedience to the One who knows us fully. The One who willingly exposed the backgrounds of the woman at the well (John 4:1–42), the woman who washed the feet of Jesus with her tears (Luke 7:36–50), and the woman who Jesus saved from being stoned to death (John 8:1–11). God knew their stories would convince me of His gentle mercy. And God knows the woman who holds this book in her hands now, sobbing because she sees herself in my story.

Oh, friends. In our hunger, why are we so willing to eat the crumbs that fall from the table? How difficult it is to wait for the promised banquet if we doubt it exists.

> *On this mountain the LORD Almighty will prepare*
> *a feast of rich food for all peoples,*
> *a banquet of aged wine—the best of meats*
> *and the finest of wines.*
> **ISAIAH 25:6**

I am not talking about physical desires, but rather the profound longing to be loved—the kind of longing that sits heavy and painful within our chest, pulling us through our beds and into the depths of the earth. Eight years of longing. An *all I've ever wanted in life is to be loved* kind of longing.

Loneliness and longing are among the enemy's favorite weapons of choice against the single mother. When we are most vulnerable, the enemy loves to arouse our hunger and entice us to a counterfeit banquet that serves nothing more than crumbs. Then, of course, he slams us with shame for stooping to such a low level.

I wish I could tell you I had it all together all of the time as a single mother—that I somehow had the power to overcome the temptation to eat the crumbs off the floor in the midst of my hunger. But that is not my story, at least not in the beginning.

Like many single mothers, I struggled in my loneliness and longing for a husband. I struggled in church as I watched men drape their arms around their wives and children during the sermon. I longed for companionship and conversation after I tucked the girls into bed at night. On Christmas morning, I wanted a husband to sit beside me and share the joy as the girls opened their presents—one who would appreciate my holiday cooking and affinity for Christmas music. I longed for someone with whom to laugh, dream, cry, and pray. Someone to hold my hand. And perhaps more than anything, I wanted a father figure for my daughters.

Loneliness led to longing. Longing led to searching. And searching led to vulnerability.

SEX AND THE SINGLE MOTHER

Do not arouse or awaken love until it so desires.
SONG OF SONGS 3:5

But what about the issue of sex as a single mother?

Because the topic is still somewhat taboo in the church, millions of Christian single mothers struggle with the complex issues of sex in silence. And some, having endured sexual abuse in their childhood, relationships, or previous marriage, struggle alone without the benefit of support or wise counsel. Considering the conflicting messages between the church and the world, it is no wonder that single mothers wrestle with shame, confusion, and desire in silent isolation.

Our world has two opposing ways in which it deals with sex outside of marriage: encouragement and shame.

Our world advocates the belief that it is natural and healthy for people to act on their sexual desires prior to marriage, as long as both partners are consensual. In addition, the media and entertainment industries perpetuate a multibillion-dollar industry that worships skin, recreational sex, and flagrant vulgarity.

On the other end of the spectrum, well-meaning Christians sometimes use shame as a way to ward off premature sexual relationships. While the Bible contains clear and consequential warnings against premarital sex, the use of Scripture to condemn, shame, or control only increases the chasm between the church and those who most need the love of God. And if abstinence programs lack the foundational teaching on value, virtue, identity in Christ, and companionship with God, we are left with a list of rules without understanding their purpose.

I suggest there remains a third way to deal with the issue of sex outside of marriage—through the lens of *grace*. The lens of grace offers a far different perspective from its counterparts because it focuses on the love of Jesus, rather than the act of sex.

Consider the ways in which Jesus interacted with women who carried sexual shame.

To the woman at the well (John 4:1–42) who was married five times and living with a sixth man, Jesus does not subject her to public ridicule. He spoke gentle words of truth in a private conversation and offered her living water. To the sinful woman who washed His feet with tears and perfume (Luke 7:36–50), Jesus offered praise for her great love and faith. And to the adulterous woman subject to stoning (John 8:1–11), Jesus saved her from condemnation before telling her to leave her life of sin.

This is the lens of grace. While the world condemned and rejected these woman, Jesus valued them. He spoke to them. Protected them and offered His grace and presence while dealing with their sexual sin.

For single mothers who adopt the world's acceptance of sex outside of marriage, the lens of grace will allow you to explore the biblical teachings about sex while being assured of God's abiding presence and unconditional love for you. Be vulnerable with Him in terms of expressing your loneliness, longing, struggles, frustrations, sin, and temptations. Read God's Word as it relates to sexual purity, understanding that He created boundaries to protect and uplift you. In the "Invitation" section of this chapter, I included key Scriptures to help you understand His best for your life. As you explore and learn, trust Him to meet you with tender grace and mercy.

For single mothers who find themselves in the torturous cycle of giving into their desires, feeling guilty, asking for forgiveness, and committing to purity, only to return to desire once again—you have a gift awaiting. Rest. Exploring the issues of sex through the lens of grace and His Word will help you to cast aside shame and allow Him to heal the issues of your loneliness and need.

And for those single mothers who faithfully walk the road of purity but may feel isolated, emotionally impoverished, and even jealous or resentful of those who give in to their desires— the lens of grace will enable you to receive the overflowing abundance God has planned for you.

So how do we obtain this lens of grace? We accept the invitation to spend significant time alone with God to develop a meaningful relationship with Him. For an extended amount of time you choose, you simply enter His presence, fully committed and free of distractions competing for your attention. Accepting His invitation to spend time together was among the best decisions I made in my life because it radically changed the way I lived and created a new legacy for my children.

*"Call to me and I will answer you and
tell you great and unsearchable things you do not know."*
JEREMIAH 33:3

The Invitation

*"Come with me by yourselves to a quiet place
and get some rest."*
MARK 6:31

Soon after I wrote my journal entry, pleading with God to show me He is enough, I heard His gentle whispers, speaking the words I always longed to hear throughout His Word.

You are mine. My love for you endures forever. You are precious and honored. I will protect you, sustain you, and uplift you. I will quiet you with my love.

Every time I opened my Bible, His words of comfort, provision, love, forgiveness, and mercy poured forth, leaving an unmistakable taste of sweetness behind.

*How sweet are your words to my taste,
sweeter than honey to my mouth!*
PSALM 119:103

No longer eating the crumbs left behind, I found myself tasting the food set before me on the banquet table, and learned it was enough to quench my hunger for love. In other words, I no longer felt desperation to fill my loneliness with a relationship because God's love became enough.

*"He has brought me to his banquet hall,
And his banner over me is love."*
SONG OF SOLOMON 2:4 (NASB)

His Word served as a foretaste of the lavish banquet that awaits. But it also served as a food of conviction. I realized that while I professed to love God, I did not *know* Him. I knew *of* Him.

Again I heard His whisper . . .

> *"Come with me by yourselves to a quiet place and get some rest."*
> **MARK 6:31**

I accepted His invitation. Instead of pouring my time and energy into a new relationship, I committed myself to spending significant time with God in prayer, in His presence, and in His Word. Days turned into weeks, and weeks turned into months and years. Two years, to be exact. Months and years of falling in love with my Savior, who first loved me.

> *We love because he first loved us.*
> **1 JOHN 4:19**

I learned that the love of Jesus covers, protects, and binds. It removed my stain of sin, presenting me holy and blameless before my Father in heaven. His perfect love became my shelter in the storm, driving out the hurricane force of fear. And if I were to lose all else but His love, I would still be filled to overflowing. Had I not taken this time to experience His love, I dare not imagine where I would be today. Most likely, I wouldn't be married to my husband, and I certainly wouldn't be writing this book.

And now, I serve as His messenger and extend the same invitation to you. Will you consider going with Him by yourself to a quiet place and rest? Will you spend time getting to know Him? *Really* know Him. Talk. Pray. Listen. Read about His life of love. Seriously consider setting aside dating and men and relationships for a period of time. They will wait. Spend days and weeks and months falling in love with your Savior instead. In doing so, you will firmly establish the single most important relationship of your life.

On page 179, you will find a "Love Letter from God." Having scoured the Bible for His words of love toward us, I put the Scriptures in a letter format to make it personal and easily accessible. Read through it and allow God to speak to your innermost longings. Print the letter off of my website and hang it on the mirror in your bathroom. Underline the Scriptures in your Bible so that every time you open it, you are reminded of His great affection for you. I can't express enough how the Word of God transformed my life.

Jesus answered, "It is written:
'Man shall not live on bread alone,
but on every word that comes from the mouth of God.'"
MATTHEW 4:4

After my divorce, I never grew accustomed to sleeping in the middle of the bed. I continued sleeping on one side, leaving the other side of the bed as an unfortunate reminder that I was alone. Every night, I read a small portion of the Bible and placed it on my nightstand just before I fell asleep. One evening, in my exhaustion, I inadvertently placed my Bible on the unused pillow beside me. The following morning, instead of waking up alone, I opened my eyes to see God's Word waiting for me. From that day forward, I fell asleep and woke with His Word beside and within me . . . and it was enough.

Reach out for him and find him,
though he is not far from any one of us.
ACTS 17:27

HOMEBUILDING 101:
The Roof

LOVE

BUILDING YOUR HOME:

1. In what ways do loneliness and longing affect you?

2. Are you currently dating or in a relationship?

3. Do you hope to marry again? If so, what are you looking for in a partner? What are you willing and able to offer?

4. What is your current stance on premarital sex, and what boundaries do you have in place? What influenced your belief system (worldly standards, biblical principles, expectations/pressure from partner, childhood upbringing, trauma, past experiences, etc.)?

5. Find an accountability/prayer partner. When exploring the biblical principles of sex and love, it is helpful to join another single mother, mentor, counselor, or small group with whom

you can discuss beliefs, Scripture, previous relationships, and choices for the future. In doing so, you will receive strength through accountability, prayer, and support.

THE INVITATION:

"Come with me by yourselves
to a quiet place and get some rest."
MARK 6:31

Consider the following suggestions.

1. Set aside a specific amount of time, free of distractions, in which you can focus solely on growing your relationship with Jesus. If you are in a serious relationship, openly discuss your needs with your partner. Together, come up with a plan that honors both your relationship and your need to spend time with Jesus. Your partner's response will tell you a great deal about his respect for your faith.

2. Buy a journal to record your prayers, thoughts, and favorite Scriptures.

3. Spend time getting to know Jesus by reading the Gospels about His life: Matthew, Mark, Luke, and John. See *Building on Solid Ground: "How to Read the Bible,"* found on page 225, or more reading suggestions.

4. Read the *"Love Letter from God"* on page 179 and underline each Scripture in your Bible. Spend some time with this letter, and let it speak to you. Write a letter to Jesus in response.

5. Talk to Jesus informally throughout each day. Using a conversational tone, speak honestly about your needs, wishes, dreams, sins, worries, and pain. Talk about your children and the legacy you hope to leave.

6. Study the roles of God. Research what the Bible has to say about God as your Father, Friend, Savior, Husband, Redeemer, Creator, Protector, Provider, and Healer. Consider how God uses these roles to meet your greatest needs.

7. Ask God about His will for your life regarding parenting, work, and relationships. Seek His answer through Scripture, prayer, and if needed, wise counsel.

8. If you have felt abandoned, forgotten, unheard, or unseen by God, talk to Him about it. If you carry doubts about His existence or love, express your concerns.

9. Ask God about His will for your life in terms of sex, dating, relationships, and marriage. When seeking His answers, be careful to not base your perception on your emotions or worldly logic. Research what His Word has to say about these issues:

It is God's will that you should be sanctified: that you should avoid sexual immorality; that each of you should learn to control your own body in a way that is holy and honorable, not in passionate lust like the pagans, who do not know God.
—1 THESSALONIANS 4:3-5

See also: 1 Corinthians 6:18, 1 Corinthians 10:13, Ephesians 5:1–20, Colossians 3:5, 1 Peter 2:11, 2 Timothy 2:22, 1 Corinthians 6:13–20, Galatians 5:16–24, Genesis 2:24, Hebrews 13:4, and Mark 10:6–9.

10. If you have suffered abuse (sexual, physical, emotional, verbal, or spiritual) or if you struggle or feel confused while exploring these issues, seek the help of a professional or pastoral counselor for needed support. Please don't go through this alone.

BUILDING A LEGACY OF FAITH: Serve others together

Beloved, if God so loved us,
we also ought to love one another.
No one has ever seen God; if we love one another,
God abides in us and his love is perfected in us.
1 JOHN 4:11-12 (ESV)

As you receive the abundant and lavish love that is in Jesus, seek out opportunities for you and your children to share God's love through service to others.

As a single mother in *need*, I didn't believe I had the time or the energy to serve. Once I began volunteering, both on my own and with my girls, I realized I had much to offer the world. My daughters learned lessons in mercy, empathy, and gratitude they would have otherwise never known. And I learned I was far stronger and more capable than I had imagined.

Serving and volunteering do not need to be a time-consuming and energy-sapping venture. Look for opportunities close to home that best fit your time, interests, energy, and talents.

Consider serving in one of the following places or brainstorm ideas with your children.

- Neighborhood. Do you have a neighbor who could use some help?
- Nursing home. Many elderly residents are lonely and would love regular visitors.
- Fire or Police stations. Bake cookies or other goodies to show your appreciation to those who serve our community.

- Animal Shelter. Shelters need food, blankets, toys, and volunteers willing to walk and socialize dogs.
- Crisis Pregnancy Center. Perhaps you have wisdom to share with new single mothers.
- Church. Numerous opportunities to serve await at your church—everything from teaching Sunday school to licking envelopes to participating in short/long-term mission trips.
- School. Are you available to volunteer occasionally in your child's classroom? Or perhaps for a special event or field trip?
- Other ideas: Adopt-A-Highway. Habitat for Humanity. Soup kitchen. Fill Christmas boxes for children in need. Knit hats for newborn babies in the hospital. Trade babysitting services with another family. Donate clothing and unused items to the needy. Host a lemonade stand or garage sale to benefit a worthy cause. Encourage another single mother.

Each of you should use whatever gift
you have received to serve others,
as faithful stewards of God's grace in its various forms.
1 PETER 4:10

Or, take in a child in need.

Quite honestly, this is not how I imagined serving God as a single mother. We were in dire need ourselves. If God had hinted at this beforehand, I would have had my list ready. *I don't make enough money. I don't receive child support, and our house is too small. I'm emotionally depleted and ill-equipped. I simply can't become responsible for another human being.*

I wasn't certain I was taking care of *my* little human beings well enough.

But God had other plans.

God sets the lonely in families . . .
PSALM 68:6

While in sixth grade, my oldest daughter, Rachel, met Lacey. The two soon became best friends and determined they were destined to become sisters. While the details of their plan ultimately failed, they achieved their goal. In a ten-year series of events that only God Himself could orchestrate, Lacey came into our hearts and home. What began as a simple act of service—bringing in a child in need—led to one of the greatest blessings of our lives. To learn more about this sweet story which eventually led to the legal adoption of an adult child, visit my website at www.michellelynnsenters.com.

LOVE LETTER FROM GOD

My Beloved,

I have loved you with an everlasting love; I have drawn you with unfailing kindness (Jer. 31:3).* *Come with me by yourself to a quiet place and get some rest* (Mark 6:31). *Along unfamiliar paths I will guide you; I will turn darkness into light before you and make the rough places smooth* (Isa. 42:16). *I tend my flock like a shepherd: I gather the lambs in my arms and carry them close to my heart; I gently lead those that have young* (Isa. 40:11).

I will instruct you and teach you in the way you should go; I will counsel you with my loving eye on you (Ps. 32:8). *I delight in truth in your inner being, and I will teach you wisdom in your secret heart* (Ps. 51:6 ESV). *Call to me and I will answer you and tell you great and unsearchable things you do not know* (Jer. 33:3). *Let love and faithfulness never leave you; bind them around your neck, write them on the tablet of your heart* (Prov. 3:3).

Cast your cares on me and I will sustain you; I will never let you be shaken (Ps. 55:22). *So do not fear, for I am with you; do not be dismayed, for I am your God. I will strengthen you and help you; I will uphold you with my righteous right hand* (Isa. 41:10). *You will call, and I will answer; you will cry for help, and I will say, "Here am I"* (Isa. 58:9). *I am your refuge and strength, your ever-present help in trouble* (Ps. 46:1). *I am your hiding place; I will protect you from trouble and surround you with songs of deliverance* (Ps. 32:7). *I will heal your broken heart and bind up your wounds* (Ps. 147:3). *I am with you as a Mighty Warrior who saves. I take great delight in you and will rejoice over you with singing* (Zeph. 3:17).

I have no beauty or majesty to attract you to me. Nothing in my appearance will cause you to desire me. I am despised and rejected by mankind, a man of suffering, and familiar with pain. But I have taken up your pain and have bore your suffering. I was pierced for your transgressions and crushed for your iniquities. The punishment that brought you peace was upon me, and by my wounds you are healed (Isa. 53:2–5).

Therefore I will now allure you. I will lead you into the wilderness and speak tenderly to you. There you will sing as in the days of your youth. In that day, you will call me your husband. I will betroth you to me forever; I will betroth you in righteousness and justice, in love and compassion. I will betroth you in faithfulness, and you will acknowledge me as your Lord (Hos. 2:14-16, 19–20). *I know the plans I have for you, plans to prosper you and not to harm you, plans to give you hope and a future* (Jer. 29:11). *Do not be afraid; you will not be put to shame. Do not fear disgrace; you will not be humiliated. You will forget the shame of your youth and remember no more the reproach of your widowhood. For I, your Maker, am your Husband* (Isa. 54:4–5). *Fear not, for I have redeemed you; I have summoned you by name; you are mine* (Isa. 43:1).

Arise, shine, for your light has come, and my glory rises upon you. Lift up your eyes and look about you. Your sons come from afar, and your daughters are carried on the hip. You will look and be radiant, your heart will throb and swell with joy (Isa. 60:1, 4–5). *I will bestow upon you a crown of beauty instead of ashes, the oil of joy instead of mourning, and a garment of praise instead of a spirit of despair* (Isa. 61:3). *I will call you by a new name* (Isa. 62:2). *I will give you a white stone with a new name written on it, known only to you* (Rev. 2:17).

Grasp how wide and long and high and deep is my love (Eph. 3:18). *Even to your old age and gray hairs I am he, I am he who will sustain you. I have made you and I will carry you; I will sustain you and I will rescue you* (Isa. 46:4). *I have searched you and know you* (Ps. 139:1). *You are precious and honored in my sight. I love you* (Isa. 43:4). *See, I have engraved you on the palm of my hands* (Isa. 49:16). *Though the mountains be shaken and the hills be removed, yet my unfailing love for you will not be shaken, nor my covenant of peace be removed, for I have compassion for you* (Isa. 54:10). *My love for you endures forever. I will not abandon the works of my hands* (Ps. 138:8).

Reach out to me and find me. I am not far from you (Acts 17:27). *Seek me. You will find me if you seek me with all your heart and with all your soul* (Deut. 4:29). *Love me, the Lord your God, with all your heart and with all your soul and with all your mind* (Matt. 22:37).

Be strong and courageous. Do not be afraid or discouraged, for I will be with you wherever you go (Josh. 1:9). *If you go up to the heavens, I am there. If you make your bed in the depths, I am there. If you rise on the wings of the dawn, if you settle on the far side of the sea, even there my hand will guide you. My right hand will hold you fast* (Ps. 139:8-10). *And surely I am with you always, to the very end of the age* (Matt. 28:20).

I am my beloved's and my beloved is mine (Song 6:3),

GOD

* This letter contains adapted Scripture quotations.

PART SIX

the
ADORNMENT

*By wisdom a house is built,
and through understanding it is established;
through knowledge its rooms are filled
with rare and beautiful treasures.*

PROVERBS 24:3-4

CHAPTER 11

IDENTITY

When I long for worth,
He is my Mirror.

Long before I divorced, I took my daughter to a neighborhood antique shop when we needed to escape the reality of our world. We wandered down each aisle, hand in hand, as I admired the handiwork of needlepoint samplers, kitchen linens, and lace. I ran my fingers across the delicate rims of china teacups and studied the workmanship of eras long past.

While Rachel felt instinctively drawn to the tin toys and faceless rag dolls, I was most intrigued with the old black-and-white photographs. Frozen eyes haunted me, begging not to be forgotten. Each had an untold story, and I searched tirelessly for a woman whose face might reflect my own. She would appear drawn and tired, old beyond her years. There would be a quiet stoicism about her, perhaps hiding the darkened truth within. Her hands would be thankful for the moment of rest the photographer offered, and her eyes would be resigned to forgotten dreams and a life she had not chosen.

But it was in a Victorian hand mirror, not a photograph, that I found this woman. The mirror sat on a dusty shelf, surrounded by handkerchiefs and perfume bottles. I picked it up and admired the intricate metalwork and beveled glass. Although the mirror was old, the reflection offered a considerable likeness, and I was charmed by its delicacy.

I turned the mirror over, expecting to see an ornate metal backing, but found something entirely unexpected. There was a second mirror, tinted blue and cracked in three places. I lifted it to my face and gazed at my reflection. A broken and discolored woman stared back at me, and for a moment, as if in a dream, I saw a picture of her soul. And it was dying.

I had finally found the woman my heart recognized.

After my daughter and I had returned to the house, I placed my $9.00 treasure on the dresser with the broken side down. The mirror served as my secret rebellion against the cruel words spoken over me, marking the start of a journey that would span two decades.

IMAGE OF SELF

For we are his workmanship,
created in Christ Jesus for good works,
which God prepared beforehand,
that we should walk in them.
EPHESIANS 2:10 (ESV)

We are God's workmanship, although rarely do we believe as such. Workmanship comes from the Greek word *poiēma*, which simply means "to make or create." The word "poem" derives from *poiēma*. But we find a deeper understanding of the word when we compare its use in another Scripture.

*For since the creation of the world God's
invisible qualities—
his eternal power and divine nature—
have been clearly seen, being understood from
what has been made,
so that people are without excuse.*

ROMANS 1:20

Here, the word *poiēma* ("what has been made") suggests that God reveals His invisible qualities, eternal power, and divine nature in His creation. *We are His creation.* His workmanship. His poem.

*Then God said, "Let us make mankind in our image,
in our likeness . . ."*

GENESIS 1:26

God created us in His image and yet, when we look into the mirror, we are more likely to examine each wrinkle, blemish, and perceived flaw. We pluck our eyebrows, exfoliate our skin, dye our hair, apply the concealer, suck in our tummies, and attempt to lose weight to feel beautiful, desired, or perhaps just acceptable.

Not surprisingly, we are just as likely to judge our inner selves with as much self-condemnation and deprecation as we use outwardly.

What do we use to define ourselves? What parameters do we use to determine our *self-worth*?

Do we wear the labels designated by society? Race. Socioeconomic level. Marital status. Political affiliation. Profession. Religion. Age.

Perhaps we define ourselves by the "ties that bind" us to our history. Do we carry words spoken over us? Curses. Blessings. Words of gratitude and belief. Words of criticism and shame.

What about our inabilities, faults, and weaknesses? Or perhaps that addiction we keep hidden, or the crushing experience that forever tainted our memory of early adulthood? Do we define ourselves by our talents, beauty, growth, and accomplishments? Our *uniqueness*? What about that *thing*? You know the one—that endearing quirk, habit, charm, or grace that makes us different than everyone else in the world. Is that the measure by which we define ourselves?

Do we carry a presumed stigma of being a single mother? Divorcee? Widow? Or unwed teen mother? Do we feel we have "welfare recipient" stamped across our foreheads?

Imagine yourself, right now, looking into an exquisite and massive gold-leafed mirror hanging on the wall of a grand palace. It offers an unflinching reflection of who you are—internal and external scars, beauty marks, quirks, warts and all.

What do you see? What words go through your mind as you gaze at your honest reflection? Imagine for a moment that someone hands you a white board marker. They instruct you to write the words on the mirror that define you best. Not sentences or your life story. Just words. What would you write? Take a moment now to write those words on the mirror image.

Who do I say I am?

For now we see only a reflection as in a mirror;
then we shall see face to face.
Now I know in part; then I shall know fully,
even as I am fully known.

1 CORINTHIANS 13:12

For many years, the mirror I used to determine my worth was horrifically cruel. I defined myself by every harsh word spoken over me—every failure, weakness, inability, quirk, and fault. I was unwanted, ugly, fat, dirty, incapable, a weight and burden, stupid, powerless, broken, used, worthless, unseen, and unloved. I was "complete nothingness."

At that point of my life, it didn't matter whether someone spoke these words over me, or whether they were self-inflicted. I wore them as clothing—tattered rags of words around my shoulders. They became my identity.

Friends quickly picked up on my poor "self-esteem" and attempted to build me up with generous doses of praise. "You are intelligent and worthwhile, Michelle." "You are a loving mother and capable of doing great things with your life." I even tried to battle the words within my mind. *I am not complete nothingness. I am valuable.*

But as soon as I heard something positive, my conditioned mind would silently argue back, *No. You are not a good mother. Remember that time you yelled unnecessarily and made your daughter cry? Remember the time you flunked Spanish in college? And don't forget that terrible thing you did. I bet God hasn't forgotten THAT.* It didn't take long before my thoughts would come into *full agreement* with the false accusations and shame.

I desperately wanted someone to believe I was beautiful and valuable because perhaps then I could believe it too. I just didn't know who could ever think of me in such a way.

My siblings and I grew up with a mother whose wisdom poured from her lips, "Your words are either life-giving or life-taking. What kind of words are you using right now?" Single momma, I ask you the same question. What words do you use to define yourself? Are they life-giving or life-taking?

If you struggle in this area as I did, find comfort knowing there is One who defines you with life-giving words of Truth. Define yourself using His mirror.

Who Does God Say I Am?

And we all, who with unveiled faces
contemplate the Lord's glory,
are being transformed into his image with
ever-increasing glory,
which comes from the Lord, who is the Spirit.
2 CORINTHIANS 3:18

Soon after I purchased the antique mirror, I had a few counseling sessions with the pastor at my church, with the hope of overcoming my negative "self-esteem." His assignment *seemed* simple, almost simplistic, and I questioned if it was worth my time. My pastor instructed me to fold a piece of paper in half lengthwise and, on the left side of the paper, write down EVERY negative thought, false accusation, and cruel word someone told me and those I thought about myself. One idea per line. He encouraged me to return, once the list was complete, for the second half of the assignment.

It took me weeks to recall and document everything I had heard and believed. It saddens me now, almost to the point of tears, as I remember the pages and pages of vicious words. *How could I have believed such slander about myself?*

When I returned with my completed list, my pastor gave me the single most important assignment of my life. For every harsh word listed, he told me to find God's counterclaim in the Bible and write it on the other side. In essence, he was teaching me how to bring my thinking into alignment with the Truth found in God's Word.

We demolish arguments and every pretension that sets itself up against the knowledge of God, and we take captive every thought to make it obedient to Christ.
2 CORINTHIANS 10:5

Focusing on God's Word provided a foundation to stand when I fought internally against hateful words. While I could argue back and forth with my thoughts and rationalizations, I couldn't argue with God's Word. I believed the Bible was unequivocally true and would never presume to challenge its authority. Now, I am obviously not advocating blind and ignorant faith. One must bear in mind the historical, political, and religious context in which Scripture is placed when studying His Word. Context is crucial when discerning the Word of God.

But because I studied Scripture in context and believed His Word was TRUTH, I no longer had to fight the battles by my strength alone. When someone told me I was "worthless," I no longer wore those words as clothing. I knew the TRUTH.

I was not worthless. I was TREASURED.

Out of all the peoples on the face of the earth, the LORD has chosen you to be his treasured possession.
DEUTERONOMY 14:2

I could no longer define myself as "unloved" or "abandoned."

See what great love the Father has lavished on us,
that we should be called children of God!
And that is what we are!

1 JOHN 3:1

No longer abandoned, I was adopted (Rom. 8:15).
No longer unsafe, but protected (2 Thess. 3:3).
No longer dirty or blemished, but cleansed (1 John 1:7–9).
No longer crippled by fear, I was courageous (Ps. 118:6).
No longer weak, I became powerful (Phil. 4:13).

I spent the next several years working on those lists, replacing each lie with the Truth of God. While the assignment felt overwhelming due to the sheer number of statements I needed to refute, it forced me to learn the profound and life-changing nature of God's Word. Once I embedded His Word into my heart and mind, my identity changed. I was no longer focused on self-image, self-esteem, self-knowledge, or self-regard. Instead, my identity centered on who I was *in Him*. This shift did not cause me to disregard my talents or abilities or dreams. It enhanced them because I knew they were God-given. Nor did this shift allow me to overlook my failures and sins. In Him, I could deal with my weakness and stand in His strength.

Therefore, if anyone is in Christ, the new creation has come:
The old has gone, the new is here!

2 CORINTHIANS 5:17

As you may have noticed, I have a deep reverence and love for Scripture. This is not because I am a writer who likes pretty words. No. God's Word is living and active, powerful beyond measure. With it, I call upon the mercy and forgiveness of Jesus. I slay the enemy and thwart his evil intentions. With God's Word, I understand my purpose and reason for being. I find the strength to parent my daughters with wisdom and dignity in the midst of hardship. And His Word serves as the mirror with which I define myself.

The heavy use of Scripture in this book is my gift to you. God's Word is far more influential than anything I could ever write. In fact, if you only take one thing with you after reading this book, please let it be a newfound love for God's Word.

All Scripture is God-breathed
and is useful for teaching, rebuking, correcting
and training in righteousness,
so that the servant of God may be thoroughly
equipped for every good work.
2 TIMOTHY 3:16-17

For many years, ill-spoken words served as the double-edged sword that pierced my side, causing old wounds to bleed again and again. Words served as the torrential wind that bowed my back.

But God's Word ...

His Word saved me.

With it, God removed the tattered rags from my shoulders and clothed me with His robe of righteousness, allowing me to straighten my back and lift my eyes to heaven once again.

I delight greatly in the LORD; *my soul rejoices in my God.*
For he has clothed me with garments of salvation
and arrayed me in a robe of his righteousness,

as a bridegroom adorns his head like a priest,
and as a bride adorns herself with her jewels.
ISAIAH 61:10

I no longer believe I am ugly, fat, stupid, powerless, worthless, and unloved.

God's Word proves I am beautiful, cleansed, capable, treasured, powerful, healed, and loved.

And I am no longer "complete nothingness."

I am a Beloved Daughter of the King and full Heir to the Kingdom.

And so are you.

We have the Scripture to prove it.

God sent the Spirit of his Son into our hearts,
the Spirit who calls out, "Abba, Father."
So you are no longer a slave, but God's child;
and since you are his child, God has made you also an heir.
GALATIANS 4:6-7

On the following page, replace some of the negative descriptions you wrote earlier with the truth found in God's Word. Refer to *Building on Solid Ground: "Identity in Christ"* on page 221 for guidance.

Who does God say I am?

And we all, who with unveiled faces
contemplate the Lord's glory,
are being transformed into his image
with ever-increasing glory,
which comes from the Lord, who is the Spirit.

2 CORINTHIANS 3:18

A New Identity

The antique hand mirror was blue and cracked in three places, opening a window into my broken soul. The mirror on the other side, however, offered a familiar likeness, and I soon came to discover it was the image of Christ in me. Trading my broken reflection for Christ's defining image was perhaps one of the most life-changing decisions I've made as a woman, because it transformed the way in which I view myself and interact with the world. This transformation continues today, purposefully orchestrated by the loving hand of God. And every once in a while, I receive a reminder of just how much I've changed or how far I have yet to go.

When preparing my home for Christmas last year, I took several items off the shelves and walls to make room for holiday decorations. Most went into boxes for temporary storage. Without much thought, I moved a metal sign to an empty nail in my bathroom. Months went by before I realized I had forgotten to return it to its original spot above the front door.

I walked into the bathroom one morning and immediately took notice of the weary bags under my eyes. Everything seemed to have aged overnight. More gray hairs. Sagging this. Drooping that. I was just about to pitch a silent fit when I glanced at the forgotten metal sign hanging in the bathroom since Christmas. It read,

Love is spoken here.

Here? In the bathroom? Somehow, I had never thought about speaking words of love and grace to myself while in the bathroom. I instinctively went to words of judgment.

Love is spoken here. Twenty years after I purchased the broken hand mirror that got me started on this journey, God continues to lead me gently into a deeper understanding of who I am *in Him.*

When my identity rests *in Him* and *in His Word,* I don't have to fear the mirror or harsh words. I know who I am and where my worth stands. *Love is spoken even here.*

I don't even have to worry about the deepening wrinkles or the uprising of gray hairs on my head. *Love is spoken here.*

> *Even to your old age and gray hairs I am he,*
> *I am he who will sustain you. I have made*
> *you and I will carry you;*
> *I will sustain you and I will rescue you.*
> **ISAIAH 46:4**

WHO DO YOU SAY JESUS IS?

While Jesus and His disciples were walking to the villages near Caesarea Philippi, He asked them a defining question.

> *On the way he asked them, "Who do people say I am?"*
> *They replied, "Some say John the Baptist; others say Elijah;*
> *and still others, one of the prophets."*
> *"But what about you?" he asked. "Who do you say I am?"*
> *Peter answered, "You are the Messiah."*
> **MARK 8:27–29**

Jesus asks the same question of us today.

> *"But what about you?" he asked. "Who do you say I am?"*
> **MARK 8:29**

If you have never considered this question seriously, take a moment now. How do you define *Jesus*? Is He merely a good teacher from whom you learn valuable lessons? Is He a fictional storybook character created to control and manipulate masses of people? What about a prophet or an important historical figure?

Do you believe Jesus is your Savior?

> *Peter answered, "You are the Messiah."*
> **MARK 8:29**

In the original Greek text, Messiah is *Christos*, meaning "the Christ, Messiah, or Anointed One." He is God's Son and the long-awaited Savior of the world. *Our* Savior.

For those of us who are Christians, we understand our identity is inextricably tied to Jesus as our Savior. This "tie that binds" is a welcome bondage, eternally connecting us to the love, grace, and family of God.

If you feel unsure about your belief in Jesus or about whether you are considered a Christian, ask yourself the following questions:

1. Do I realize that my sin eternally separates me from God unless an atoning sacrifice is made?

> *All have sinned and fall short of the glory of God.*
> **ROMANS 3:23**

> *For the wages of sin is death, but the gift of God is eternal life in Christ Jesus our Lord.*
> **ROMANS 6:23**

2. Do I believe that Jesus, the Son of God, spared me from this eternal separation by offering Himself as an atoning sacrifice for my sins through His death on the cross?

> *For God so loved the world that he gave*
> *his one and only Son,*
> *that whoever believes in him shall not*
> *perish but have eternal life.*
>
> **JOHN 3:16**

3. Have I confessed my sins before God and asked for His forgiveness?

> *If we confess our sins, he is faithful and just and*
> *will forgive us our sins and purify us*
> *from all unrighteousness.*
>
> **1 JOHN 1:9**

4. Have I declared Jesus as my Lord and received His free gift of salvation?

> *If you declare with your mouth, "Jesus is Lord,"*
> *and believe in your heart that God raised him from the*
> *dead, you will be saved.*
>
> **ROMANS 10:9**

> *"Believe in the Lord Jesus, and you will be saved—you*
> *and your household."*
>
> **ACTS 16:31**

If you answered yes to these questions, you are a Christian and can rest in the full assurance of His salvation. If you remain unsure about your beliefs, know that God remains ever close to you. He will walk beside you as you grow in your knowledge and acceptance of Him. But just to warn you, He is unrelenting in His pursuit of us.

So great is His love, He will never tire of drawing us close to Himself.

HOMEBUILDING 101:
The Adornment

IDENTITY

BUILDING YOUR HOME:

1. What words do you typically use to define yourself? If you have not yet done so, make a list of these words.

2. From where or whom do these defining words originate? Society? People? Yourself? God?

3. Are any of these defining words bound to an old wound that needs healing? Do you need to remove any "ties that bind"? If so, refer to chapter 6.

4. Take some time to explore God's Word in relationship to your identity. Replace each harsh word with the TRUTH of God. Who does He say you are? Surround yourself with His

definition of you. Write these Scriptures on your mirrors, re-frigerator, and sticky notes. Read them repeatedly until you have embedded God's Word into the fabric of your being. For assistance in finding these Scriptures, refer to *Building on Solid Ground: "Identity in Christ"* on page 221.

5. Think about the roles of God in our lives. He is our Creator, Father, Savior, and Friend; Healer, Provider, and the Lover of our souls. How does knowledge of His roles affect your identity?

BUILDING A LEGACY OF FAITH: Identity as family

Having rented for the past fourteen years, I've often dreamed of painting the walls any color I choose—preferably in reds and yellows, reminiscent of the Tuscan villages I hope to visit someday. I've wondered how it might feel to press my daughters' hands into the wet concrete, leaving their imprints on our porch as indelible as they are on my heart. I long for a home that reflects our identity as a family—our eclectic sense of style, passion for the arts, and love for God and one another.

On a Mother's Day years ago, my daughters discovered a way to temporarily showcase who we were in our little rental home. The girls were playing quietly outside, a little too quietly, so I checked on them. Sure enough, I found Gabrielle playing in a large hole filled with mud. Believing she was in trouble, she wiped her hand on the wooden fence behind her, leaving a per-fect and beautiful handprint. This, of course, inspired Rachel, who immediately looked to me for permission. Soon we were all covered in mud up to our elbows as we painted the fence with dozens of mud handprints.

The handprints dried in the sun and permanently adhered

themselves to the fence. I don't remember if we ever made it to church that Mother's Day. But the handprints remained throughout the year, offering an endearing reminder of who we were as a family each time I looked through the window. For as long as we lived in that home, we went outside on Mother's Day and put new mud prints on the fence. It became a tradition.

Despite the hardships and struggles, your time as a single mother has potential to go down in your history as the sweetest years of your life. Embrace it. Celebrate your family. Make mud handprints. Take photographs. Hang a family portrait. Cherish this precious time, for it is a gift of God.

And our children's hands and fingers grow all too soon.

For you created my inmost being; you knit me
together in my mother's womb.
I praise you because I am fearfully and wonderfully made;
your works are wonderful, I know that full well.
My frame was not hidden from you when
I was made in the secret place,
when I was woven together in the depths of the earth.
Your eyes saw my unformed body;
all the days ordained for me were written in your book
before one of them came to be.

PSALM 139:13–16

PART SEVEN

SETTLING IN

"But blessed is the one who trusts in the LORD,
whose confidence is in him.
They will be like a tree planted by the water
that sends out its roots by the stream.
It does not fear when heat comes;
its leaves are always green.
It has no worries in a year of drought
and never fails to bear fruit."

JEREMIAH 17:7–8

CHAPTER 12

THE BLESSING

"I will plant them on their land,
and they shall never again be uprooted
out of the land that I have given them,"
says the LORD your God.

AMOS 9:15 (ESV)

I still ache for a home of my own.

Now having moved houses thirty-one times in forty-six years of life, I long to send my roots deep within purchased soil and plant myself firmly, never again to be uprooted. I want to stretch my branches wide in my chosen spot under the sun and soak up its summer warmth.

We yearn for all kinds of roots. A home. Family. Heritage. We want to know where and to whom we belong. This yearning is a holy longing, purposed in our hearts by God that we might look to His Son as our Savior and Unseen Companion and root ourselves in Him.

So then, just as you received Christ Jesus as Lord,
continue to live your lives in him, rooted and built up in him,
strengthened in the faith as you were taught,
and overflowing with thankfulness.
COLOSSIANS 2:6-7

A potted red geranium sits on my desk, reminding me of where I've come from and where I'm going. As I look at it now, I'm embarrassed to admit that it shows serious signs of neglect. Dry soil. Brown, shriveled-up leaves. One stalk of dying flowers. I have no fear for my plant, though. Upon closer look, I notice several baby leaves emerging from the stem, and a sprout I suspect will grow into the next mini-bouquet of red flowers. With a little water and pruning, my geranium is sure to thrive.

As a single mother, I always kept at least one pot of red geraniums throughout the year. In the summer, they graced my doorway, sharing their tiny plot of land with petunias, alyssum, and an occasional zinnia. In the fall, I brought my geraniums inside the house and placed them in a sunny window, where they continued to bloom throughout our cold Colorado winters.

I'm not sure when I brought home my first pot of geraniums. Perhaps I purchased them as a young single mother because I longed for flowers, but felt foolish to buy myself a bouquet. My affection for the flower undoubtedly came from my Papa. Long before he adopted me as his granddaughter, Papa and Nana lined the front of their house and driveway with dozens and dozens of red geraniums each year, much to the delight of their family and neighbors. And for twenty years after Nana's death, Papa continued their beloved tradition as a testament to her. After his death, my parents moved into his home and continued the decades-long gardening project.

As long as I had one pot of geraniums, I knew I was home. They survived year after year, home after home, connecting me to something much larger than myself.

After years of growing these beauties, I've come to understand their greatest asset. Geraniums are remarkably hardy. They can survive a month of neglect, withering to nothing but a leggy stalk and a few dead leaves. Once watered and pruned to only a couple inches high, the plant will eventually return with lush, green leaves and vibrant flowers. Geraniums live through multiple repottings, the first unexpected frost of the year, scorching sunshine, deep shade, drought, overwatering, and breakage due to the occasional tipped pot or harsh weather. They were a perfect plant for this busy single momma.

At some point, however, geraniums became a symbol not only of home, but of my life as a single mother. We both carry a strong will to survive. In a geranium, this will to survive is set forth in the fiber of its being. My will comes as a gift of God.

But we have this treasure in jars of clay
to show that this all-surpassing power is from God
and not from us.
We are hard pressed on every side, but not crushed;
perplexed, but not in despair;
persecuted, but not abandoned;
struck down, but not destroyed.
We always carry around in our body the death of Jesus,
so that the life of Jesus may also be revealed in our body.
2 CORINTHIANS 4:7–10

Our secret lies below the surface. As long as a geranium has viable roots, it will live. Even if the plant breaks, destroying all the roots, a clipping from the stem placed in water will grow new roots. In the few times I have lost a geranium plant, it was always due to a root issue.

As long as we remain rooted in the love of our Unseen Companion, we know we are not alone. Rooted in Him, we know our children will thrive, and our house will stand strong, long after we are gone. For we are not just building houses to live in, single mommas; we are building legacies from which our children and our grandchildren will build.

You began this journey with me as I stood in the desert wasteland years ago, with my young girls clinging to the hem of my skirt. You watched as I unsuccessfully tried to rebuild from the discarded and broken remnants of my life. You saw as the Unseen Companion drew close and helped me rebuild my home. You were there as I laid the foundation on the Rock that is Jesus and as I pieced together the framework of my home, strengthened by His companionship, provision, healing, rest, and strength. You observed how secure I felt as He built His walls of protection and peace around us. As the girls and I sat in His presence, you saw Him raise His banner of love over us, securing it as a roof over our heads. And as He adorned my house with things of beauty, you saw me peek into the mirror to see how my reflection had changed.

Here it is, fourteen years later. You and I are old friends now. You sit on the white porch swing in front of my house and sip tea as we chat. Your children play in the grass beneath the old oak tree, whose twisted branches remind us of the storms of long ago. And while you tell me about your house renovation project, you watch me water the pots and pots and pots of red geraniums on the porch. You don't ask me why I have so many flowers. You know.

Our time together goes by all too quickly, and as you gather your children to start heading home, you are not surprised when I hand you a pot of red geraniums. "I've been growing these for you," I say. "Put them on your front porch to welcome you home each day." We hug and say our long goodbye.

Flowers appear on the earth; the season of singing has come . . .
SONG OF SONGS 2:12

With your geranium in hand, you walk with your children down the driveway and notice another visitor arrive. You turn and watch for a moment as her children immediately run to play under the old oak tree. The young woman walks up the steps, one by one, with a hand on the rail to steady herself. And as she sits and rests on the porch swing, you know she came for a potted geranium and to hear the old story about the Unseen Companion.

I pray that out of his glorious riches
he may STRENGTHEN YOU with power
through his SPIRIT in your inner being,
so that CHRIST MAY DWELL IN YOUR
HEARTS through faith.
And I pray that you,
being ROOTED and ESTABLISHED in LOVE,
may have power, together with all the Lord's holy people,
to grasp how WIDE and LONG and HIGH and DEEP
is the LOVE of CHRIST,
and to know this LOVE that surpasses knowledge—
that you may be filled to the measure of
all the FULLNESS of GOD.
EPHESIANS 3:16–19 (emphasis added)

Be strong and courageous.
Do not be afraid;
do not be discouraged,
for the LORD your God
will be with you
wherever you go.
JOSHUA 1:9

BUILDING on SOLID GROUND

Scriptures for the Single Mother

"If you abide in my word, you are truly my disciples, and you will know the truth, and the truth will set you free."

JOHN 8:31–32 (ESV)

BALANCE

2 Corinthians 1:8–9
Psalm 62:2
Matthew 19:26
Psalm 40:1–2
2 Corinthians 4:8–9
Matthew 7:24–27

COMFORT

Isaiah 66:13
2 Corinthians 1:3–4
Psalm 119:76

COMPANIONSHIP

Psalm 139

Matthew 28:20

Joshua 1:9

John 15:13

John 15:15

Joshua 1:5

DIRECTION

Psalm 32:8

Proverbs 3:5–6

James 1:5

Psalm 77:19

FORGIVENESS

Psalm 25:16–18

2 Corinthians 13:11

Matthew 6:12–13

HEALING

Amos 9:11

Isaiah 58:6

Hosea 11:3–4

Psalm 34:18

Luke 4:18–19

Psalm 103:2–4

Psalm 147:3

Galatians 5:1

HOME

Amos 9:11

Psalm 127:1

Psalm 27:4

Psalm 61:4

Psalm 23:6

Psalm 84:4

Psalm 91:1

2 Corinthians 6:16

Ezekiel 37:27

Psalm 90:1

John 14:23

Acts 17:26–28

1 Corinthians 3:11

2 Corinthians 5:1

Isaiah 28:16

Luke 6:47–49

Matthew 7:25

Proverbs 9:1

Psalm 122:7–9

Song of Songs 2:4

Proverbs 24:3–4

HOPE

Romans 5:3–5

Psalm 27:13–14

Romans 15:13

Isaiah 49:23

IDENTITY

Ephesians 2:10
1 Corinthians 13:12
2 Corinthians 5:17
2 Corinthians 10:5
Romans 12:2
Colossians 3:10
Deuteronomy 14:2
2 Corinthians 3:18
Isaiah 61:10
James 1:22–25
Revelation 2:17
Isaiah 62:2–5

LOVE

John 3:16
1 John 4:11–12
Mark 12:30
Song of Songs 3:2
Romans 8:38–39
Song of Songs 2:4
Hosea 2:19
Isaiah 54:4–5
Zephaniah 3:17
1 John 3:1

PEACE

Philippians 4:6–8
1 Peter 5:7
Psalm 46:10
John 14:27

PERSEVERANCE

Galatians 6:9

2 Corinthians 4:7–9

James 1:2–4

James 1:12

2 Chronicles 15:7

Romans 12:12

PROVISION

Isaiah 46:4

2 Corinthians 9:8

Philippians 4:19

Matthew 7:7

John 16:23–24

Philippians 4:6

PROTECTION

2 Samuel 22

Isaiah 41:10

1 John 4:4

Psalm 27:1

Psalm 57:1

Psalm 46:1

PURPOSE

Romans 8:28

Psalm 138:8 (ESV)

Proverbs 19:21

Jeremiah 29:11–14

Ephesians 4:1

REST

Isaiah 40:28–31

Genesis 2:2–3

Leviticus 23:3

Isaiah 30:15

Psalm 23:1–3

Deuteronomy 33:12

Psalm 91:1

Proverbs 3:24

Psalm 4:8

Psalm 3:5

Matthew 11:28–30

Mark 6:31

Jeremiah 6:16

Hebrews 4:9–10

Psalm 91:4–5

STRENGTH

2 Chronicles 15:7

Psalm 27:14

Philippians 4:13

Philippians 4:11–13

2 Corinthians 4:7–9

Psalm 73:26

Isaiah 40:29–31

Ephesians 6:10

2 Corinthians 12:9–10

Psalm 31:24

Isaiah 30:15

TEMPTATION

Job 8:13–15
Hebrews 2:18
Hebrews 4:15–16
1 Timothy 6:11–12
Matthew 6:13
Matthew 26:41
1 Corinthians 10:13

WISDOM and DIRECTION

Psalm 32:8
Proverbs 3:5–6
Isaiah 42:16
Isaiah 30:21
Philippians 3:13–14
Psalm 77:19

For a printable list of these scripture verses please go to:
www.michellelynnsenters.com

BUILDING on SOLID GROUND

Identity in Christ

Therefore, if anyone is in Christ, the new creation has come: The old has gone, the new is here!
2 CORINTHIANS 5:17

I AM FORGIVEN.

Ephesians 1:7–8
Colossians 1:13–14
Romans 8:1

I AM ADOPTED.

Romans 8:14–17
Galatians 4:6–7
Ephesians 1:4-6
John 1:12–13

I AM PROTECTED.

Psalm 121:7–8
Psalm 12:5
2 Thessalonians 3:3

I AM A NEW AND BEAUTIFUL CREATION.

2 Corinthians 3:18
Romans 12:2
Ephesians 2:10
Psalm 139:13–16
Isaiah 62:2–4

I AM A FRIEND OF GOD.

John 15:15

I HAVE GREAT PURPOSE IN MY LIFE.

Jeremiah 29:11
Romans 8:28
Philippians 1:6
John 10:10

I AM STRONG IN HIM.

Philippians 4:13
Ephesians 6:10
2 Timothy 1:7

I AM NOT ALONE.

Matthew 28:20
Deuteronomy 33:12

I AM ACCEPTED.

John 6:37
Romans 12:1
Romans 14:18

I AM VALUABLE.

Isaiah 43:4
Deuteronomy 7:6

I AM BLESSED.

Ephesians 1:3
Numbers 6:24–26

I AM LOVED.

John 3:16
Romans 8:38–39
Hosea 2:19–20
Isaiah 54:5
Jeremiah 31:3

For a printable list of these scripture verses please go to:
www.michellelynnsenters.com

BUILDING on SOLID GROUND

How to Read the Bible

*All Scripture is God-breathed and is useful for teaching,
rebuking, correcting and training in righteousness,
so that the servant of God may be thoroughly equipped
for every good work.*
2 TIMOTHY 3:16–17

Q: I'd like to read the Bible, but it is overwhelming. Should I start at the beginning?

A: The Bible is a collection of "God-breathed" writings that include thirty-nine books in the Old Testament and twenty-seven books in the New Testament. Some people start at the beginning of the Bible and read all the way through. This disciplined approach tells the overall story of God and His people. When I was a single mother, however, I lacked the time necessary to read the Bible cover to cover. Instead, I focused on the books of the Bible that offer direction, hope, and tangible help.

SUGGESTIONS

1. Choose a translation that is both inspiring and comfortable to read. I prefer the New International Version (NIV) and the English Standard Version (ESV) The ESV offers a "word for word" or literal translation of the original Greek and Hebrew text. The NIV, on the other hand, strikes a balance between "word for word" and "thought by thought" translation. Both versions are well respected and easily understood. Consider purchasing a "Study Bible" or a "Life Application Bible" in the translation of your choice. "Study Bibles" provide a deeper understanding of Scripture through notes on historical and cultural context, Hebrew and Greek definitions, maps, charts, and cross-references to other books of the Bible. "Life-Application Bibles," on the other hand, include notes that help readers apply God's Word to their lives.

2. Using a fine tip pen, underline EVERY verse that speaks to you. Write notes in the margins. Underlining will cause your eyes to focus on the Scripture time and time again, allowing it to embed in your heart.

3. Purposefully engage with God and His Word while you read. Ask yourself the following questions and pray for God's discernment:

- What does this Scripture reveal about the character of God?
- What message or truth is conveyed in this passage?
- Talk to God about your reaction to His Word. Do you feel comforted, inspired, or convicted? Challenged or strengthened? Are you angry, confused, or defensive?

- Ask God how you should apply this Scripture to your life.

4. If you are an auditory learner, supplement your reading with digital recordings of the Bible. If you are a visual learner, document your learning through words and art in a journal.

WHERE TO BEGIN: GOSPELS

To learn about Jesus, read the Gospels of Matthew, Mark, Luke, and John in the New Testament. While all the Gospels recount the life, ministry, death, and resurrection of Jesus, each book offers a unique perspective and focus.

MATTHEW: Originally written for the Jews, this Gospel provides a connection between the Old and New Testaments by focusing on Jesus as the long-awaited Messiah. Key Scriptures: Beatitudes (Matt. 5:3–12), Sermon on the Mount (Matt. 5:1–7:29), The Greatest Commandment (Matt. 22:34–40), and The Great Commission (Matt. 28:16–20).

"Come to me, all you who are weary and burdened,
and I will give you rest.
Take my yoke upon you and learn from me, for I am
gentle and humble in heart,
and you will find rest for your souls. For my yoke is
easy and my burden is light."
MATTHEW 11:28–30

MARK: Written for the Gentiles, the Gospel of Mark offers a quick and succinct overview of the life of Jesus, focusing on the actions of Jesus. Key Scriptures: Fishers of Men (Mark 1:17), Proclamation of the Risen Jesus (Mark 16:6)

Love the Lord your God with all your heart
and with all your soul
and with all your mind and with all your strength.
MARK 12:30

LUKE: This Gospel is famous for its eloquent portrayal of the birth of Jesus. Beginning with His birth and ending with His ascension into heaven, Luke gives a detailed account of the life of Jesus, emphasizing His humanity, compassion, forgiveness, and love. Key Scriptures: Birth of Jesus (Luke 2:1–20), Prophecy of Isaiah Fulfilled (Luke 4:16–20), and Do Not Worry (Luke 12:22–34).

Today in the town of David a Savior has been born to you;
he is the Messiah, the Lord. This will be a sign to you: You
will find a baby wrapped in cloths and lying in a manger.
LUKE 2:11-12

JOHN: The Gospel of John offers a contemplative and even poetic depiction of Jesus, focusing on Him as Messiah. Key Scriptures: Word Became Flesh (John 1:1–5), God So Loved the World (John 3:16), Woman at the Well (John 4:1-42), Jesus Is the Way (John 14:5–7), and Peace I Leave (John 14:27).

For God so loved the world that he gave
his one and only Son,

> *that whoever believes in him shall not perish*
> *but have eternal life.*
> **JOHN 3:16**

Old Testament scriptures that prophesy about Jesus include:

- Birth of Jesus: Isaiah 7:14, Isaiah 9:6–7
- Ministry of Jesus: Isaiah 61:1–2 (compare to Luke 4:18–19)
- Death of Jesus: Isaiah 53, Psalm 22

WHERE TO BEGIN: OLD TESTAMENT

PSALMS: One of the most beloved books of the Bible, Psalms is a collection of 150 poems, hymns, and songs. Covering the broad spectrum of emotion and experiences, Psalms serve as a model of prayer to God.

> *By day the LORD directs his love, at night*
> *his song is with me—*
> *a prayer to the God of my life.*
> **PSALM 42:8**

PROVERBS: In the Book of Proverbs, King Solomon offers practical advice on money, family, friends, temptation, emotions, character, work, responsibility, honor, and speech. Praising wisdom as more "precious than rubies" (Prov. 8:11), Proverbs shows a stark contrast between those who are wise and those who are not. Because there are thirty-one short chapters in this book of wisdom, many people make a habit of reading one chapter per day for a month.

The fear of the LORD is the beginning of knowledge,
but fools despise wisdom and instruction.

PROVERBS 1:7

ISAIAH: This prophetic book predicts both the judgment of man (Isa. 1:1–39:8) and the promise of restoration through the coming Messiah (Isa. 40:1–66:16). Using both poetry and prose, Isaiah offers comfort and hope for all who suffer, particularly single mothers.

"Do not be afraid; you will not be put to shame.
Do not fear disgrace; you will not be humiliated.
You will forget the shame of your youth
and remember no more the reproach of your widowhood.
For your Maker is your husband—the LORD Almighty
is his name—
the Holy One of Israel is your Redeemer; he is called
the God of all the earth.
The LORD will call you back as if you were a wife
deserted and distressed in spirit—
a wife who married young, only to be rejected,"
says your God.
"For a brief moment I abandoned you, but with
deep compassion I will bring you back."

ISAIAH 54:4-7

GENESIS: The first book of the Bible begins our story with God. Genesis contains several of the most iconic stories of the Old Testament, including: the Creation, Adam and Eve, the Fall of Man, Cain and Abel, Noah and the Flood, Tower of Babel, Abraham, Sodom and Gomorrah, Isaac, Joseph and His Coat of Many Colors, and Jacob and His Twelve Sons.

In the beginning God created the heavens and the earth.
GENESIS 1:1

WHERE TO BEGIN: NEW TESTAMENT

GOSPELS: Matthew, Mark, Luke, and John, as mentioned above.

THE EPISTLES: The Epistles include 21 "letters" in the New Testament (from Romans to Jude), each written by an apostle or a family member of Jesus. The Epistles offer blessings, address issues, and provide instruction for holy living. While all the Epistles are reasonably short in length and beneficial to spiritual growth, consider starting with the following:

ROMANS: This letter by Paul to the church at Rome offers the best explanation of salvation and grace.

If you declare with your mouth, "Jesus is Lord,"
and believe in your heart that God raised him from
the dead, you will be saved.
ROMANS 10:9

EPHESIANS: In his letter to those in Ephesus, Paul exhorts believers to grow in spiritual discipline, maturity, unity, and strength.

Therefore be imitators of God, as beloved children.
And walk in love, as Christ loved us and
gave himself up for us,
a fragrant offering and sacrifice to God.
EPHESIANS 5:1-2 (ESV)

PHILIPPIANS: While imprisoned in Rome, Paul wrote a letter to believers in Philippi, encouraging them to take on the character of Jesus and persevere through trials and suffering.

I can do all this through him who gives me strength.
PHILIPPIANS 4:13

ACKNOWLEDGMENTS

I thank my God every time I remember you.
In all my prayers for all of you, I always pray with joy.
PHILIPPIANS 1:3–4

Thank you, God, for redeeming my story. You are my Unseen Companion, and in You I've found my home.

To my dear husband, Jeffrey. Thank you for loving me enough to endure my incessant storytelling and subsequent retellings. In doing so, you helped me find my voice and courage to write. You were worth the long wait. I love you.

To my three beautiful daughters. Who would I be without you girls? Rachel, thank you for making me a momma and teaching me to live for someone beyond myself. I will always protect you. Gabrielle, I've always felt thankful for your sweet and silly demeanor, but it is your profound faith in God that inspired me to keep my eyes lifted toward heaven. And Lacey, you've had my heart since the first day we met. Thank you for choosing me to be your Momma. And oh, my beautiful grandbabies. Thank you for grandbabies.

Thank you, Mom and Dad, for leaving a legacy of faith and love worth following.

To my siblings, Nichole, Paul, and Brittany. We are among the lucky ones.

To Grandma Ann. Everyone needs a cheerleader. Thank you for being mine. Oh, how I love and miss you.

To Judy Dunagan, my acquisitions editor and friend. Thank you for breathing God's Word over my life and work.

Thank you to Elizabeth Newenhuyse, my editor. Your gentle nudge made me a better writer. I have yet to work on my speed.

To my dear sisters in Christ, Alicia and Cheri, for walking, carrying, pushing, and praying me through to the other side. I can never thank you enough.

To Mom—Joanna Senters. You read every word and encouraged me along the way. Thank you.

To my writing confidants: Ana, Sandy, Scoti, Sharon, Shelly, and Stacy. Thank you for graciously sharing your knowledge, friendship, wit, and love for words.

To my high school choir director, Pat Dalton. Though you disguised it as music, you were among the first to engrave God's words deep into my heart, and there they remain. Thank you.

Liesl, I may never know if you were a dog or an angel in disguise this side of heaven, but thank you for protecting us. You're my girl.

Nancy Karpenske, thank you for drawing me back within the folds of God's love and introducing me to single mothers' ministry. You've influenced me more than you know.

My dear friends Lynn and Steve Brown, thank you for believing in this work and coming alongside me in ministry. God answered many of my prayers when you came into my life.

To Fr. David Duprey. Thank you for teaching me how to find my identity in Christ alone. That assignment changed everything. Thank you, also, for encouraging me to "seal" my children each night. The blessing continues.

Thank you to the great women of my life, for your prayers, example, and encouragement. I love you all: Elizabeth, Rebecca, Naomi, Rhonda, Sandy, Chanel, Alyssa, Brittany, Chris, Kate, Judi, Karin, Haley, Francine, Cathryn, Brandi, Arisbeth, Katherine, Dorissa, and Sue.

Thank you New Life Church, Woodmen Valley Church, and Lifebridge Church for loving single mothers.

And to all the DEAR SINGLE MOMMAS I've known and have yet to meet, this book is for you. Thank you for entrusting me with your stories. I feel privileged and blessed to walk beside you. I love you.

BEING A MOM IS HARD,
but it doesn't have to be lonely.

Also available as an eBook.

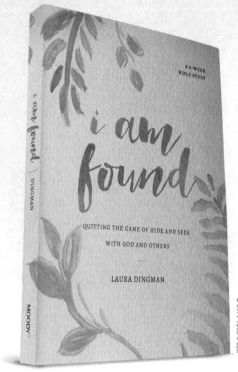

Discipleship Resources

978-0-8024-1382-6   978-0-8024-1343-7   978-0-8024-1340-6

Moody Publishers is committed to providing powerful, biblical, and life-changing discipleship resources for women. Our prayer is that these resources will cause a ripple effect of making disciples who make disciples who make disciples.

Also available as eBooks

MOODY
Publishers™

From the Word to Life